Sweet Tea Please

Sweet Tea Please

✦

Recipes and Recollections from Coastal North Carolina

Vicki Prescott

Sweet Tea Studio

iUniverse, Inc.
New York Lincoln Shanghai

Sweet Tea Please
Recipes and Recollections from Coastal North Carolina

iUniverse books may be ordered through booksellers or by contacting:

iUniverse
2021 Pine Lake Road, Suite 100
Lincoln, NE 68512
www.iuniverse.com
1-800-Authors (1-800-288-4677)

Because of the dynamic nature of the Internet, any Web addresses or links contained in this book may have changed since publication and may no longer be valid.

The views expressed in this work are solely those of the author and do not necessarily reflect the views of the publisher, and the publisher hereby disclaims any responsibility for them.

Cover Design by Vicki Prescott

ISBN: 978-0-595-47299-4 (pbk)
ISBN: 978-0-595-91577-4 (ebk)

Printed in the United States of America

Special Dedication and Thanks

With heartfelt appreciation I dedicate this work to the one woman who is responsible for the writing of this book. That special lady is, Velma Marie Harper Scott, my Grandmother, who just turned ninety years old this year and from whom I still continue to learn. She still has untold recipes, countless stories, and innumerable lessons about life, love, forgiveness, faith, understanding and being happy. I am looking forward to learning more from her as the years pass.

Her family has been, and remains, her richest asset. She is a shining example of how the treasures of a simple life can bring happiness and satisfaction well beyond the meaningless acquisitions that weigh us down. She has taught me to face each day and each person with a smile. What she means to me goes well beyond any words that I might write. She is, and shall always be, my inspiration.

Special Acknowledgment

Brandi Prescott-Robertson
Kristen Prescott

Photograph Credits

Brandi Prescott-Robertson
Kristen Prescott
Michelle Peele
From archives of Velma Harper Scott

Dedication

This book is dedicated to the four ladies below, my grandmothers. I was one lucky girl. I was able to spend lots of time with my two grandmothers, and two of my great-grandmothers. They were all wonderful women and I cherish the memories I have of them. All had different cooking styles and all were great cooks. I can remember my favorite dishes from each of them and I have shared many of them in this book.

Nothing can trigger a memory quite like food and no one can prepare it quite as well as a grandmother. These women started me on that journey, the love of cooking, and gave me cherished memories to share with future generations. Thank you.

(From Left to Right)
Velma Marie Harper Scott
Maternal Grandmother
Margie Falstina Lee Harper Dowty
Maternal Great-Grandmother
Lotha Metrude Fornes Banks Gause
Paternal Grandmother
Fannie Elizabeth Roberts Fornes
Paternal Great-Grandmother

"The only real stumbling block is fear of failure. In cooking you've got to have a what-the-hell attitude."

—*Julia Child*

Contents

Preface

Why "Sweet Tea Please"? Well, the south has undergone quite a few changes over the last few decades. We are changing from sleepy little fishing villages and farming communities, to tourist destinations and retirement havens. One subtle, but nevertheless, heartfelt change for us, is that we now have to ask for sweet tea. Can you imagine? Never before would any true southerner have dared to ask, "sweet or un-sweet?" It was just a given. Tea is sweet, it is served over ice, and if you want to be a little fancy, with a lemon slice, but always cold and always sweet. I mean really folks, would you ask someone if they wanted sweet or un-sweet lemonade. No, because lemonade is made with sugar, and in our eyes, and in our hearts, so is tea. We were weaned on sweet tea, and if the truth be known, some of us even had it in our bottles. It is as much a part of us as our southern drawls and front porches. We have it for dinner and supper and all times in between. We entertain with it, we sip it when we're happy and we sip it when we're sad. Sweet tea **is** the south, and it wouldn't be the same without it.

When I started researching and writing for this book, memories of people and their food kept popping up. It's funny how so many of our memories are associated with food. Just seeing a grapevine or fig bush in someone's yard reminds me of the wonderful preserves my Grandma Velma made every year. Sundays and fried chicken, summertime and strawberries, your love of pork chops, the smell of fresh cooked ham. These are sweet memories for me.

I have been cooking and enjoying it since I was tall enough to stand at the stove. I loved to sit and watch my Grandmothers do anything in the kitchen. Canning, baking a cake, or skimming cream off the top of a cooled pan of cow's milk. There was something about the whole process of creating recipes and cooking for my family that I just treasured. Cooking for me was art and creation and love, all packed together.

When did this fascination with food start? I'm not really sure, I mean I've always loved to eat good food. I do remember my Grandmama Velma had this set of cookbooks that had these big, beautiful, color photos of food to go along with the recipes. Her sister had given them to her for Christmas one year. She knew that Grandmama liked to cook and I guess she thought she would love to try out some of those fancy recipes, with exotic sounding names. Now she should have known that Grandmama had her own way of cooking and to tell you the truth, I know that she didn't ever use one single recipe out of those fine looking books. How do I know? I know because she kept those beautiful books in a closet in her bedroom, and kept the recipes that she did use in a little drawer in the kitchen. Of course most of the time she never even looked at a recipe. Now back to those fancy cookbooks. Instead of the story books that the other grandkids would choose to look at during nap time, I fell asleep thumbing through those books and longing to taste all of that fine-looking food! I was lulled to sleep with big colorful pictures of perfectly cooked vegetables and luscious chocolate cakes. Maybe my obsession with cooking started then.

I am thankful that I was raised here, on the beautiful east coast of North Carolina. There are so many things you can learn from farmers and fishermen and those who live off the land and sea. Things you can't get from school or books. You grow up learning things that stay with you for life, like how to go chicken neck crabbin' and how to cook 'em up when you got home; how to make a tar-plaster for your chest when you got a bad cold; how to catch your own shrimp, head 'em and cook 'em, all in the same day; how to dig potatoes; take in tobacco; go cane pole fishin'. These things were daily occurrences for us and I never realized, until years later, that other people might not be living and experiencing that laid back life like we were. We did all kinds of things that maybe someone growing up in a city wouldn't or couldn't do or just didn't have the opportunity to do. You know, important things like sittin' in the grass and making necklaces out of clover, building forts back in the woods, swimming in the creek; riding around in the back of your daddy's pick-up truck; eating a tomato right out of the garden; front porch singing; and being a *sweet tea girl (more about that later)*.

I'm thankful for those fishermen and farmers and their wives who taught me so much about life. I'm thankful for the mamas' and grandmamas' and daddys' and granddaddys' who taught us to be respectful, to say yes ma'am and no sir, who gave us discipline with a switch from the back yard when we needed it, (I didn't feel that way at the time) who taught us to wash our hands and bless our food before we ate. I am thankful for the culture, the laid back life and of course, that good southern food.

"In the South, the breeze blows softer ... neighbors are friendlier, nosier, and more talkative. (By contrast with the Yankee, the Southerner never uses one word when ten or twenty will do) ... This is a different place. Our way of thinking is different, as are our ways of seeing, laughing, singing, eating, meeting and parting. Our walk is different, as the old song goes, our talk and our names. Nothing about us is quite the same as in the country to the north and west. What we carry in our memories is different too, and that may explain everything else."

—Charles Kuralt in "Southerners: Portrait of a People"

Acknowledgements

Where oh where do I begin? Let me start with my girls, Brandi Prescott-Robertson, Kristen Denise Prescott and Lena Marie Robertson. Brandi and Kristen, my daughters, helped me so much. They told me which recipes I just had to include, and also which ones to leave out. They helped me with colors, designs, (they are very opinionated), and supported me throughout the entire project. My perfect granddaughter, Lena Marie, was there to make me smile and laugh and think of the future. I wanted her to be able to have recipes that came from her grandmother, great-grandmother, great-great grandmothers, and great-great-great grandmothers. Thank you to my beautiful girls.

To my mama, Susie Banks, for always telling me that I could do anything I set my mind to do. She has always been there to strengthen and push me and give me the confidence to do what she already knew I had in me to do. Thank you Mama.

To my friends, for giving me encouragement and staying on my behind to finish. I sometimes have a habit of hopping from one project to another and losing interest, but they helped me stay focused, and gave me inspiration without even knowing it. So, after nearly two years I finally finished it. Thank you to my "girl-friends"—Linda Little, Michelle Peele, Mary Ann Bruno, Patsy Heath, Tonya Cedars, Michelle Shields and Miriam Prescott.

Finally, to my husband of thirty years, Bobby Prescott. Thirty years? We are gettin' old baby. Thanks for answering all of my questions about crabs and shrimp, for sampling recipes and having the courage to tell me when it just wasn't quite good enough for the book. Thank you for being such a wonderful husband (he is going to use this, when I get mad at him about something). Thank you for making me laugh every day and for being my best friend.

The Southern Staple
Sweet Iced Tea

8 cups of cold water (2 quarts)
1 1/4 cups of sugar
3 Family Size Luzianne™ Tea Bags

Bring the cold water to a full boil, add the tea bags, and remove from heat.

Let steep for at least 10 minutes

Add sugar to a 2 quart pitcher

Pour tea over the sugar.

Serve over ice with lemon slices

Of course everybody has their own way of making iced tea, and I'm sure they're all good. If you ask twenty different women from the south how to make iced tea you will get twenty different answers. I make at least one pitcher of tea every day and this is the way I make it, strong and sweet.

I always start with cold water and always use Luzianne™ Tea. Don't try to use a fancy tea for sweet iced tea. It's not supposed to be fancy, just good.

I NEVER refrigerate my tea. It gets dark and I don't like the taste after it has been in the refrigerator. I just can't imagine going a day without sweet tea.

"She loves sweet tea better than Peter loved the Lord."

—Dick Banks (my Daddy) (1938-1997)

Tea Tips

Always start with cold water. Cold water has more oxygen in it than warm or hot water, which will leave you with a flat tasting tea.

When tea is heated, tannins, which are the natural compounds that color tea leaves, are released. The heat helps dissolved the tannins and you have a nice clear tea. When you refrigerate tea, those tannins separate, and the tea will get a cloudy, murky look (and to me, a funny taste). So don't refrigerate your tea.

If for some reason you have to refrigerate your tea and it gets cloudy add about ¾ cup of boiling water to it. That should take care of those tannins and clear it up.

Don't add ice to the hot pitcher of tea. Put the ice in your glass.

Always use a glass or ceramic pitcher that can take the heat. A metal or plastic pitcher sometimes can take on other flavors and can leave an oily film on the tea.

The tea is only going to be as good as your water. If you have really hard water try using bottled water to make your tea. Also remember that the ice you are pouring it over can also affect the taste of the tea.

Please don't buy that powdered tea stuff. I mean really, what's in it? Is there even real tea in there?

I promise you, it's not that hard to make a great, fresh pot of iced tea. So get busy.

If you are cold, tea will warm you. If you are too heated, it will cool you. If you are depressed, it will cheer you. If you are excited, it will calm you.

—Gladstone, 1865

Something About Ingredients

I'm not here to endorse name brands BUT there are certain things that are a must.

Tea. As I said previously, I think that Luzianne™ makes the best iced tea. (But watch out Luzianne™ I could develop my own brand!)

Mayonnaise. Duke's™ or Hellman's™ always! No substitutes! Salad dressing is not mayonnaise, it's not even close. I don't know what's in it, but it will cause a HUGE difference in the taste of recipes.

Butter. REAL butter. I never use margarine or that whipped stuff that is supposed to taste like REAL butter. It doesn't. And what is it anyway, oil, water, air and food coloring? Yuck. Put your trust in the cows, not scientists.

Salt. Kosher. It makes a big difference. Use it and you'll see. You will never use iodized salt again.

Seafood. Buy the freshest possible. Fresh frozen is next best.

Vegitables. Again, buy local, fresh vegetables from your local farmers market if at all possible. Maybe even change your menu to use what's available that day. Fresh vegetables are always better than frozen and frozen vegetables are always better than canned.

Cocoa. Hershey™. It's not that I have a problem with other chocolate, and I do use some fancier chocolates on occasion, but that's the kind my Grandmama always used and for that authentic southern taste you can't beat it.

Flour. Unless otherwise stated, I use Martha White™ All Purpose (AP) Flour. For biscuits I always use Martha White™ Self Rising (SR) Flour.

Who am I?
I'm a Sweet Tea Girl

What's a *Sweet Tea Girl*? She's a girl from the south, or at the very least, a girl who yearns to be from the south, and sweet iced tea has to be her all time favorite refreshment (even if a little bourbon is added in). I do have lots of girlfriends from "up-north" who are quite acceptable as *Sweet Tea Girls*, because after all, it's all about attitude right? *Sweet Tea Girls* are not like those southern debutants, queens, or princesses you hear about. We do not want a crown, we proudly wear our *Sweet Tea Girl* ball caps. We are strong, southern girls (we will still be called girls when we are approaching ninety) who don't take a heck of a lot of crap, can do just about anything and aren't afraid to do it, we don't wait around for the world to come to us, we go out and grab it by the tail. We can be tough as nails and we can be sweet as sugar, it just all depends on what (or who) we're dealing with that day.

Me? I was born in North Carolina, to a young mother and father who were continually being told they didn't know nothing about raisin' no baby. Which was probably true, but somewhat of a ritual among southern grandparents of the day. Canned Pet™ milk filled my bottle, a little Karo™ syrup added in if I was being fussy, and later on a little sweet tea. My Grandmama chewed up cornmeal dumplings, spit them out and fed them to me, just like a mama bird with her young. That's how it was done, and sometimes still is.

I grew up on a dirt road, went barefoot most of the year, and my Grandmama made all my clothes until I reached high school. I've used an outhouse, a slop jar and took baths in a galvanized wash tub. I went to church every Sunday, freshly bathed and in no less than my best dress and Sunday shoes.

I've been to hog killin's, milked cows, rode rowdy horses, mucked stalls, plucked eggs from underneath a chicken, had a pet sheep and at least one dog in the house since I was born.

4

I've eaten, squirrel, rabbit, deer, bear, quail and doves, all shot by my Daddy or Granddaddy. Some of which I liked, some of which I didn't. I've drunk sassafras tea made from roots we dug up in the woods and chewed pine sap pulled off a pine tree, just for fun.

(Me and my sister at Minnesott Beach, just a few years back.)

The "beach" (which was really the Neuse River) was our haven. Swimming and crabbing off the dock filled most of our week-ends. Yep, that's me with that mass of brown curls and those cat-eye glasses.

I grew up chicken neck crabbin, fishing in the creeks, shrimping in the rivers. I know what a trot line is, a trawl door, a tail bag, a sook and a peeler.

Our beach was the creeks and the mighty Neuse River. I've picnicked, driven boats, tried to water ski, been skinny dippin' and spent the majority of my spare time on the water.

I've planted tobacco beds, set out tobacco plants, handed tobacco, looped tobacco to a stick, filled barns with tobacco, took out barns of tobacco, and graded tobacco. I've dug potatoes, picked every vegetable known to man, shelled thousands, upon thousands, upon thousands, of peas and pecans.

I've taken too many doses of Castor Oil and Castoria to remember, had tar plasters stuck to my chest, taken a tablespoon of sorghum molasses everyday to "keep my energy up".

I've had big hair, driven loud, fast cars, sung in church, drunk a little whiskey, and have been known to cuss upon occasion.

I learned all the things a good southern girl needs to know from my kin. I learned to work and sing, from my Daddy. I learned to be polite, use my manners, and flirt when necessary, from my Mama. I learned to cook from my Grandmama, and when to be quiet from my Granddaddy.

I drink sweet tea; eat boiled peanuts, love collard greens, pork, grits, red velvet cake and sweet potatoes.

I can also dress up, talk sweetly and be a real southern lady when and if I need too. There's no doubt about it, I'm *Sweet Tea Girl* through and through, and mighty blessed to be one.

"The biggest myth about Southern women is that we are frail types—fainting on our sofas … nobody where I grew up ever acted like that. We were about as fragile as coal trucks."

—Lee Smith

Appetizers, Finger Foods, Nibblers, & Beverages

Whatever you want to call it …
Little bites of this and that,
Spreads and Dips
and something good to wash it down with.

"Happy and successful cooking doesn't rely only on know-how; it comes from the heart, makes great demands on the palate and needs enthusiasm and a deep love of food to bring it to life."

—Georges Blanc, from 'Ma Cuisine des Saisons'

"The Tray"

Still today when my girls are coming for a visit, they will call and say "Mama, have a tray ready for us."

A tray of what? Well, it might be anything from cheese and crackers to crab dip, but to our family it's that "tray" you make about four or five o'clock in the afternoon to tide you over until supper time. Or it's that tray you make when you get some unexpected company and want to be social, but you don't have enough stuff in the house for a full meal.

Somewhere along the way I started making a "tray" of appetizers every evening just before "Daddy got home." It might just be cut up fruit and cheese or whatever I could throw together out of the pantry or refrigerator. (I came up with some great concoctions doing that!) Anyway, you know how it is, once you start something, and they get used to it, well, you just can't stop, and then after a while, it becomes routine. It's just the way we do things now, a little something before supper time.

My girls always made sure a tray was ready when they had friends come over and they really got good at being able to look in the pantry and the refrigerator to come up with different things to put on "the tray". Sometimes we even had "trays" for our supper! It's fun to eat little bites of lots of different things.

So we now have this tradition that we always have to have a tray. Oh, I know it's turned into a tradition because I called my daughter the other night and asked her what she was doing and she said "Oh I'm just making a tray" … and there was no further explanation necessary.

Crab Artichoke Spread

This is standard fare at our house. I make it for special occasions and for just sitting around watching a ball game. It's really great stuff and is good the next morning on toast. Even if you think you don't like artichokes, you will like this. For fancy events serve it in a chafing dish. It's sure to be a hit.

1 1/2 cups mayonnaise
2 (14-ounce) cans artichoke hearts, drained (not marinated)
1 cup Parmesan cheese
1 package cream cheese
1 teaspoon black pepper
1/4 cup fresh chopped parsley
1 or 2 teaspoons hot sauce (depends on how hot you want it)
1/2 to 1 pound backfin crabmeat (free of shell)

Preheat the oven to 350°.

Mix all ingredients together.

Pour all into a 2-quart baking dish.

Bake for 30 minutes, or until golden and heated through.

(You can also make it without the crabmeat if you don't have it on hand.)

Pecan Cheese Crackers

Cheese wafers are always served at southern gatherings. I love pecans so I decided to put some pecans in the recipe and I really think they are much better.

Make sure that you use extra sharp cheese in this recipe. If you make it with mild cheese.... well just don't.

1 pound shredded extra sharp cheddar cheese
2 sticks butter at room temperature
3 cups self-rising flour
1 teaspoon cayenne pepper
2 cups finely chopped pecans

Preheat the oven to 350°.

In a food processor or stand mixer, blend together the shredded cheese and the butter until well combined.

Add all of the other ingredients and mix until everything is well blended.

Separate the dough into four portions and shape into the size you want your crackers. I usually shape mine in logs that are about an inch and a half thick.

Wrap in plastic wrap and put in the refrigerator for at least an hour.

Slice into 1/4 inch rounds.

Bake on cookie sheet until crisp. About 12 minutes.

Heavenly Ceviche

This is a fantastic ceviche using fresh seafood, a perfect dish for coastal North Carolina. It's probably not something, (no, it's definitely not something) my Grandmothers would have made, but in our area, with all the fresh seafood, I think it's a must. The lime juice cooks the seafood, and it's a wonderful dish that can be used as an appetizer or a salad with fresh greens. This has to be made at least four hours in advance, so plan ahead.

1 pound shrimp, peeled and deveined and cut in half or in thirds if large
1/2 pound scallops, cut in half (if small leave whole)
1 pound fresh, sushi grade tuna (cut into 1 inch chunks)
8 limes, juiced
6 ripe firm tomatoes, seeded and diced
3 green onions, chopped
1 cucumber, peeled, seeded, small dice
2 jalapeno peppers, seeded and minced
1/2 cup chopped fresh cilantro (or fresh parsley if you don't like cilantro)
2 tablespoons freshly chopped dill weed
2 tablespoons good, fragrant extra virgin olive oil
1 avocado, diced
1 tablespoon hot sauce
Salt and pepper to taste

Wash all of the seafood with cold water and place in a large mixing bowl.

Squeeze the juice from all of the limes over the seafood, making sure all the seafood is coated.

Stir in the tomatoes, green onion, cucumber, peppers, cilantro, dill, olive oil and avocado.

Cover and refrigerate for at least 4 hours.

Before serving taste and season with salt and pepper as desired.

Carolina Shooters

These were a big hit at Bobby's 60th (sorry baby, you really don't look it) birthday party. They are great served as an appetizer in shot glasses.

Fresh shucked oysters
Red Sauce (see recipe)
Hot Sauce
Vodka or Beer

Place a fresh shucked oyster in a shot glass

Top with a teaspoon of red sauce. Add a dash (or two or three) of hot sauce

Fill shot glass with either Vodka or Beer. Shoot it!

Oh Baby!!

Southside Salsa

1 (15-ounce) can black-eyed peas
1 (15-ounce) can black beans
1 (8 1/2-ounce) can whole kernel corn
1 jar of your favorite salsa
1/4 cup fresh chopped cilantro (or parsley if you don't like cilantro)
1/2 cup Italian salad dressing
1 clove of minced garlic

Drain the peas, beans and corn and combine with the remaining ingredients.

Serve with tortilla chips.

Crabmeat in Red Sauce

I was having a party and was planning to make a hot crab dip, but I got side tracked with something and ended up running way behind schedule. Ten minutes before everyone was to arrive I still needed to make the crabmeat appetizer. I went to my refrigerator and grabbed ingredients for a red sauce and mixed it all together with the crabmeat. I put it out on a beautiful crab platter surrounded by lemon slices and crackers. Everyone just raved about it. Not even a teeny bit was left.

Sauce:
1 cup catsup
2 teaspoons Worcestershire
Juice from one lemon
1 tablespoon hot sauce
1 heaping tablespoon of horseradish

1 pound jumbo lump or backfin crabmeat
2 tablespoons fresh chopped parsley

Mix all of the sauce ingredients together until well blended.

Fold in the crabmeat.

Sprinkle parsley over the top.

Chill.

Serve with crackers or over lettuce as a salad.

Crab Puffs

These crunchy little "puffs" are sure to be a hit at your next gathering.

1/2 pound fresh crabmeat
1 cup of biscuit mix
1/2 teaspoon salt
1/2 teaspoon garlic powder
1 tablespoon fresh chopped parsley
1 teaspoon grated lemon zest
1/4 cup milk
1 egg
2 tablespoons fresh lemon juice
1 teaspoon Worcestershire sauce
1 tablespoon hot sauce
Oil for frying

Mix all of the ingredients together except the crabmeat. Make sure this mixture is well blended.

Fold in the crabmeat.

Drop the batter by teaspoonfuls into hot oil. Fry for about 30 seconds or until golden.

Serve these while hot.

Jalapeño Shrimp Poppers

These taste great and look great too.

12 peeled and deveined large fresh shrimp
12 jalapeño peppers
6 bacon slices, cut in half lengthwise

Cut a slit lengthwise in each jalapeño pepper.

Remove seeds and place one shrimp inside of each pepper.

Wrap each pepper with 1 bacon piece, and secure with a wooden toothpick.

Place in a baking pan and broil 6 to 7 minutes on each side, or until bacon is cooked.

If you prefer these can be cooked on the grill.

Serve with Red Sauce, Champagne Sauce or Dill Sauce

"Having the world's best idea will do you no good unless you act on it. People who want milk shouldn't sit on a stool in the middle of a field in hopes that a cow will back up to them."

—Curtis Grant

Feta Cheese Spread

I love Feta Cheese and this is a great spread that's quick to make

1 (8-ounce) package cream cheese, softened
2 (4-ounce) packages crumbled feta cheese
2 tablespoons heavy cream
10 fresh mint leaves
1 or 2 garlic cloves, minced

Process all ingredients together in food processor or stand mixer until smooth.

Serve with toasted sour dough or French baguette.

Deviled Eggs

6 large eggs

2 tablespoons mayonnaise

1 teaspoon prepared mustard

1 1/2 tablespoons sweet pickle cubes

Dash of salt

Dash of pepper

Paprika

Place eggs in a single layer in a saucepan; add water to cover. Bring to a boil, boil for 3 minutes, cover, remove from heat, and let stand 15 minutes. Drain water and peel under cold running water. Slice eggs in half lengthwise, and remove yolks.

Mash yolks with mayonnaise, relish, mustard, salt, and pepper; stir well. Spoon yolk mixture into egg whites and sprinkle with paprika.

Picnic Pinwheels

I make these a lot to carry on the boat. You can make them ahead and they don't get soggy like some sandwiches do.

8 ounces cream cheese at room temperature
1 cup sour cream
1 cup grated cheese (use your favorite cheese)
1/2 cup chopped green olives
1/2 cup chopped green onion
1 teaspoon garlic powder
2 dashes of hot sauce
Fresh spinach leaves
Thinly sliced, turkey, ham, roast beef, corned beef (choose whichever you like best or use a combination)
Flour Tortillas

Combine the cream cheese, sour cream, cheese, olives, green onions, garlic powder and hot sauce. Blend until smooth.

Spread the cheese mixture over a tortilla and layer on spinach, your choice of meats and roll up tightly. Repeat until you have run out of ingredients.

Refrigerate the tortillas at least 4 hours.

Remove and cut into 1 inch slices.

Sweet Chicken Bites

This is a great little bite size appetizer.

3 or 4 chicken breasts, cut into 1 inch cubes
1 can sliced water chestnuts
1 pound bacon
2/3 cup brown sugar
1 tablespoon soy sauce
2 teaspoons hot sauce

Preheat the oven to 350°.

Slice all of the bacon in half.

Wrap a piece of bacon around a piece of chicken and water chestnut.

Secure with a toothpick.

Mix together the sugar, soy sauce and the hot sauce.

Dredge the wrapped chicken in the sugar mixture and place on a greased sheet pan or broiler pan.

Bake 30 to 35 minutes or until the bacon is crispy.

Bourbon Baked Brie

1/4 cup brown sugar
1/4 cup chopped pecans
1 tablespoon bourbon
1/2 (17.3-ounce) package frozen puff pastry sheets, thawed
1 7 or 8 inch round of Brie

Preheat oven to 400°.

Stir together the brown sugar, pecans and bourbon and set aside.

Roll out puff pastry on a floured surface. Spread brown sugar-and-pecan mixture in a 6-inch circle in center of the pastry sheet. Place the Brie on top of pecan mixture.

Wrap pastry around Brie, pinching to seal tightly, on a baking sheet, folded side down.

Bake for 25 minutes or until pastry is lightly brown.

Serve warm with French baguette slices, fruit and crackers.

Grandmama's Jar Milkshakes

Milkshakes before blenders? My Grandmama made these for me as a special treat and I never forgot how great they tasted. I made them for my girls and they still love them. So make these for your kids or grandkids or yourself!

1 Mason jar with tight fitting lid   1 teaspoon vanilla

1 1/2 cups of whole milk   Ice

2 tablespoons sugar

(For chocolate add 1 tablespoon of unsweetened cocoa powder).

Put all of the ingredients in the quart jar, add the ice and put on the lid. Shake the jar until the milk becomes frothy and ice cold. Pour into a tall glass and serve. Boy is that good!

Feel Better Creamy Cocoa

This cocoa was a real treat for us. Mama or Grandmama made it a lot in the winter or whenever we had a cold. It's so much better than the powdered stuff.

3 tablespoons cocoa (unsweetened)	2 1/2 cups milk
3 to 4 tablespoons sugar	Pinch of salt
1/2 cup water	1 teaspoon vanilla

Mix the cocoa, sugar and water together and brig to a boil. Turn heat to low and add milk and salt. Cook until steamy hot. Remove from heat and add vanilla.

Annie Ruth's Lemonade

Miss Annie Ruth worked in a restaurant we owned some years back. One hot day she decided she would make some lemonade for the folks working in the kitchen. Well from then on we asked Miss Annie Ruth to make us lemonade everyday. It was the best. The little pieces of lemon that she cut up and added are a special treat. We love this lemonade and after you make it you won't ever think about buying that powdered stuff again.

8 to 10 large lemons
1 1/2 cups water
1 3/4 cups sugar (more if you want)
6 to 8 cups cold water

Slice the lemons in half and squeeze out all of the juice, which should yield about 1 1/2 cups

Cut up two of the lemons in small pieces and set aside

In a saucepan add 1 1/2 cups of water and the sugar and bring to a boil.

In a two quart glass pitcher add the lemon juice, water and sugar mixture, the lemon juice, additional water, salt and reserved lemon pieces. Stir well.

Serve over ice.

"Ecstasy is a glass of tea and a piece of sugar in the mouth"
—Alexander Pushkin (1799-1837)

The Ultimate
On The Rocks Margaritas

This is by far the best margarita you will ever taste. I know it sounds a little strange with the beer, but believe me, you will love it. I got the original recipe for this drink from a girlfriend of mine and just decided to add a little Triple Sec.

Note from Vicki

Don't put this in a blender, on the rocks only. (Blending the beer and 7-Up is not a good idea unless you just like cleaning up a mess). Don't use any other kind of beer except Corona™, and don't use any other soda except 7-Up™.

1   12 ounce can of frozen limeade concentrate
1   12 ounce can of water (use limeade can for measuring)
1   12 ounce bottle of Corona™ beer
1   12 ounce can of 7-Up™
1   12 ounce can of Tequila
6   ounces Triple Sec

Mix all of the ingredients in a large pitcher and chill.

Serve over ice in salt rimmed glasses. OH BABY!

The Girls'
Beach Week-end Cosmos

Me and a couple of my girlfriends worked on this recipe while staying at the beach for a week-end. We worked really hard all week-end at trying and sampling different concoctions but we decided this was the best.

2 ounces Vodka
1 ounce Cointreau
1/2 ounce fresh squeezed lime juice
1 ounce of cranberry juice

Shake the ingredients with ice in cocktail shaker. Strain into martini glass. Have fun.

Mojito Mama's

If you have an abundance of mint in your garden this is the drink for you. A bit of work but it's really refreshing and very tropical.

2 (or 3) ounces good Rum
1/2 fresh lime cut into small pieces
12 medium sized mint leaves
1 ounce water
2 teaspoons sugar
Club Soda

Put the lime, mint, water, and sugar into the bottom of a sturdy pint glass. With a wooden spoon or muddler, break up and mash the mixture until the sugar has dissolved and the mint and lime are broken up.

Add the Rum and fill with ice. With a metal shaker cover the glass and shake until well mixed. Pour into a tall glass and add club soda to fill.

"Southern Family Names"

Christmas, Easter, Birthdays and Sunday's were all about family when I was growing up. Family has always been so important to me. I loved to sit around and listen to the older folks tell stories about my ancestors. Only after I was a little older did I realize that some of the names that had been handed down through generations were really unusual and some I have never heard of anywhere else.

On my mama's side…. Uh-oh, I guess I had better stop and talk about "sides" here. Now this is very important in southern culture. "Now was that on ya mama's side or ya daddy's side?" As a child you will always hear comments like, "Yeah that boy is as dumb as a stick, he's from ya Daddy's side of the family." As southerners our lineage follows us, good or bad, throughout our lives. We can't escape it. Every grandmother or aunt can tell you who is who, further back than you might care to know.

Okay, let's get back to the names. My very favorite family name of all time, is on my mama's side. Even though I love it, my daughters thanked me for not carrying on the tradition of Oklahoma Maude. Don't you just love it? Oklahoma Maude is definitely my favorite name of all time and I just don't think it can be topped. Also on my mama's side was my Great Grandmama, Margie Falstina (ever heard that one before?) Falstina … I tried to find out where this name originated but I haven't been able to find anything. Then Margie Falstina names her daughter, and my great aunt, Hazel Mayfield. I have never heard of anyone named Mayfield either! I love these women for being the original thinkers that they were. On my Daddy's side there was my great-grandmama Fanny, who we called Mammy but Fanny was a very popular name back then. Both of my husband's Grandmothers were named Fanny. My grandmother was, Lotha Metrude, I bet you never heard that one before either.

The men on mama's side, on the other hand, didn't have such unusual names, although they were all, from what I've heard, quite the band of characters. Men who made an impression one way or another. You weren't going to forget Mac, Alton Campbell, Riley, and Thaddeus.

The fellas were pretty good on daddy's side too, Ervin Jesse, Mack Dallas. My daddy's father, Mack Daniel's mother's name was Lula and his daddy was Artis. I kind of like both of those names too.

So maybe we should go back to some of those old names … a bunch of girls named Fanny, Falstina Metrude and Oklahoma Maude instead of Jessica and Megan.... Well, on second thought, maybe not.

*Standing on the far left is my Great Step-Grandmother Oklahoma Maude,
my Granddaddy Alton stooping down, my Uncle Terry is the smiling little
boy in front, my Mama with that head full of black curls and Grandmama
Velma there on the end.
(I think she still has that hat).*

Yes, my family picked plenty of cotton. No not me! I'm not THAT old!

I have heard lots of stories about picking cotton though. And my Grandmama
gets so mad now when she sees how much cotton the combines leave in the field.
She said she would have been skinned alive had she left that much cotton on a
plant. "Would you just look at that—what a waste!" I myself, think it's kind of
pretty. Like white flowers peaking out of a field of brown.

"Go to the Doctor?"

The only time you were taken to the doctor was if there was a fear of death or a lot of blood present. There was a "cure" for everything. I guess that most of them worked because I'm still here. Here's a list of some of the things that "cured me". There are a lot more, but this is really a cookbook and I didn't want to gross anybody out with things about dogs licking wounds … you understand.

- My Grandma Lotha made me take two big tablespoons of sorghum molasses every morning. She said it would give me energy throughout the day.

- In my mama's mind, Castor Oil was a cure for just about anything. In my mind, I could get better in a hurry with just the "threat" of having to take a dose.

- If you had a chest cold, one of two things would happen. You had to take a teaspoon of sugar with one or two drops of kerosene in it, or you had to wear a tar plaster. A tar plaster was made by taking an old piece of cotton and smearing on a concoction of pine tar and Vicks salve, pin it to an undershirt and put on the shirt so it's tight to the chest. You smell to high heaven, but your chest cold will go away.

- If you got a bad rash they would take some flour and scorch it and then rub it on the rash. This does work pretty well.

- Put tobacco out of a cigarette or wet snuff on a bee sting.

- If you got ringworm you had to tape a penny to the place where the ringworm was and in a couple of days it would be gone.

- Iodine and Mercurochrome was put on just about everything, cuts, scrapes, bites, all of us kids in the neighborhood always had those reddish brown telltale splotches all over us.

- Hot, sweet lemonade, with a little bourbon mixed in, was given to stop a cough. (I still use this one).

Breads
&
Breakfasts

Corn Bread
Muffins
Biscuits and More

"All sorrows are less with bread"

—Miguel de Cervantes, Don Quixote

Mama Tine's Buttermilk Biscuits

Mama Tine was my mother-in-law and a fantastic cook. This is about as close as I can come to her biscuits, which she made every day, and in the early years, twice a day (Boy have we gotten lazy.) She always made her biscuits by hand, she never rolled and cut them out and they were all always the exact same size! (That's an art in itself!). Making a good biscuit is all in the touch and I watched her many times make these biscuits. I've tried to write down exactly how she did it … so give it a try … maybe you have the touch.

2 cups self-rising flour
1/4 cup lard
(she didn't have a recipe, just told me about the size of a walnut, so I figure that's about 1/4 cup)
2/3 to 3/4 cup buttermilk

Preheat oven to 475°.

Put flour into a large bowl. Make a well in the center and put in the lard and a little of the buttermilk. Gradually work the flour into the well and keep adding the buttermilk until you have it all incorporated and have a soft dough. Knead gently only two or three strokes. (Might have to add a little flour).

Gather enough dough to make about a 2 inch biscuit roll in hands and place biscuits on a baking sheet.

For softer biscuits have the sides touching each other and if you want crisper biscuits don't let the sides touch.

Bake for 10 to 12 minutes, or until tops are golden brown.

Note from Vicki

Lard. Mama Tine used the *lard in the orange box* for her biscuits. It's still there in the grocery store. Just look over there by the Crisco™. Yes you can use a solid vegetable shortening instead but those biscuits are not going to taste as good.

Clabber?

What is clabber? Your Granddaddy didn't have a cow did he? Clabber is unpasteurized milk (straight from the cow) that is allowed to sour and thicken naturally. My Grandmama's always had a jar of it in the refrigerator. And you will never, ever, taste a biscuit that brings you closer to your southern childhood as one made with clabber. It gave you a kind of sour, moist tasting biscuit. Clabber wasn't just used for making biscuits either. Granddaddy would eat a bowlful with sugar sprinkled over the top, sort of the same thing as plain yogurt today. So how are you going to make Clabber Biscuits if you don't have clabber? Well, that's a good question. You can use plain yogurt but it's not exactly the same ... and soured milk, well, it isn't the same at all.... I guess you need to find someone with a cow.

Lard?

What is lard? Lard is an animal fat produced from rendering the fat portions of the pig. Southerners know lard by that bright orange box that their mama's kept in the pantry or the ice box. My Maternal Grandmothers always used Crisco for their biscuits and my Paternal Grandmothers and Bobby's mother always used the *lard in the orange box*. It really will give your biscuits that distinctive southern taste.

Wood?

My Grandma Velma told me that she hasn't eaten a decent biscuit since she stopped cooking with wood (and that's been a while ago). I can just imagine what they might have tasted like, the tartness from the clabber, the flakiness from the lard, and that slight smoky taste from the woodstove. Smothered in butter that was just made the day before and grape preserves from the grapevine out back. I imagine that would be about as close as you are going to get to heaven on earth.

Clabber Biscuits

2 cups self rising flour
2 tablespoons lard
Pinch of baking soda
3/4 cup clabber

Preheat oven to 450°.

Pour the flour into your bread bowl and cut in the lard. Then mix in all of the clabber to form a soft dough.

Knead only a few seconds or you will have tough biscuits. Form the biscuits by hand or roll out and cut about ¼ inch thick (you will need to add a little more flour when forming the biscuits or rolling them out).

Bake them in a hot oven for about 7 to 10 minutes depending on your oven.

Cheese Biscuits

I see all these recipes now for cheese biscuits where the cheese is grated and mixed up in the dough. That is not a cheese biscuit where I come from.

Take your favorite biscuit recipe and make the dough. Then cut up some good cheddar cheese (I use sharp or extra sharp cheddar) into about ¾ of an inch chucks. Form your dough around the cheese and close it up good so the cheese won't run out. Bake as you would your regular biscuit.

Remove from the oven. Break it open … see that melted cheese running out? Now that's a cheese biscuit.

Quick Yeast Rolls

There's nothing much better than the aroma of fresh yeast rolls baking. You don't have to do a double rise on these so you can get them on the table much quicker.

2 packages active dry yeast
1/4 cup lukewarm water
1 tablespoon sugar
1 1/2 cups buttermilk
2 tablespoons sugar
1/2 cup vegetable, canola or corn oil
4 1/2 cups AP flour
1 teaspoon salt
1/2 teaspoon soda
3 tablespoons melted butter

Preheat oven to 400°.

Mix the yeast with the water and 1 tablespoon sugar. Set aside.

Heat the buttermilk to lukewarm and add to the 2 tablespoons sugar, oil and the yeast mixture.

Add the flour, salt and soda to the buttermilk mixture and knead for about 5 minutes.

Form into rolls and put in baking pan.

Brush with melted butter and set in a warm place to rise for at least 30 minutes.

Bake for 8 to 10 minutes depending on the size of your rolls.

Jesus Bread

Okay, we all know it's really Pita Bread, but my girls always called it Jesus Bread so there you go. They started calling it Jesus Bread because that's the kind of bread they cut up for communion at our church.

When Bobby was growing up he lived right down the street from a Lebanese family and he still talks about going to their house and what wonderful bread their mother was always baking. Bread which he loved. He thought it was amazing that the bread would puff up like a balloon and then go back down.

No, I wouldn't call it a southern thing, but we southerners have learned to love all kinds of different foods.

And no, this is not a recipe on how to make pita bread. It's about what to do with it once you have gone to the store and purchased it.

- In a flat iron skillet, pour a little oil and over medium high heat, slightly brown the bread on both sides. Remove from the heat and slice into triangles. This is great as an appetizer with cheese, dips or fruit or also just as the bread with a meal. I fix pita bread like this at least once or twice a week.

- In a flat iron skillet, pour a little oil and over medium high heat, slightly brown the bread on both sides. Remove from the heat and slice in half. Stuff with grilled chicken pieces, sour cream, feta cheese, shredded lettuce, cucumber slices and diced tomatoes. This is a frequent meal at our house and we call it "Chicken and Pita". It's fantastic.

Grandma Lotha's Cracklin' Bread

What the heck are cracklins? Well it's the little bite size remains of the pork that have been rendered from the fat during a hog killin. Sort of a cousin to pork rinds, but cracklins have a little meat them. You can still buy them at some grocery stores. I know you can get them at a Piggly Wiggly if there is one in your area. It really gives a different flavor and a crunch to regular cornbread. Cracklin Cornbread and a pot of old navy beans with ham hocks mmmmmmm.... don't knock it if you haven't tried it.

1 1/2 cups plain corn meal (not self rising)
1/2 cup all purpose flour
2 teaspoons salt
1 teaspoon soda
1/2 teaspoon baking powder
1 cup buttermilk
1/2 cup of cracklins

Preheat oven to 375°.

Mix corn meal, flour and other dry ingredients.

Add buttermilk and mix well.

Fold in cracklins.

Pour into a greased iron skillet and bake until golden brown.

> "If more of us valued food and cheer and song above gold, it would be a merrier world."

> —J.R. Tolkien (1892-1973)

Baby Corn Muffins

These are delicate little muffins that will almost melt in your mouth. Great when served with soups, chowders, seafood and you can also serve them as an appetizer.

1 egg
1/2 cup milk
1/2 cup butter
1 8 ounce can of cream style corn
1 cup AP flour
1 cup yellow cornmeal
1 tablespoon sugar
1 tablespoon baking powder
1 teaspoon salt

Preheat oven to 425°.

Mix the eggs, milk, butter and the corn together.

Stir in the dry ingredients and mix well.

Spoon the mixture into small muffin tins to about ¾ full.

Bake for 15 to 20 minutes

Overnight French Toast Casserole

1 loaf French bread
8 large eggs
2 cups half-and-half
1 cup milk
2 tablespoons sugar
1 teaspoon vanilla
1/4 teaspoon ground cinnamon
1/4 teaspoon ground nutmeg
1 dash salt

Topping:
1 cup butter
1 cup packed light brown sugar
1 cup chopped pecans
2 tablespoons light corn syrup
1/2 teaspoon ground cinnamon
1/2 teaspoon ground nutmeg

Slice bread into 1-inch slices. Arrange slices in a buttered 9 by 13-inch flat baking dish in 2 rows, overlapping the slices.

In a bowl, combine the eggs, half-and-half, milk, sugar, vanilla, cinnamon, nutmeg and salt and beat with whisk until well blended. Pour mixture over the bread, making sure all are covered with the mixture. Spoon some of the mixture in between the slices. Cover with foil and refrigerate overnight.

The next day, preheat oven to 350°.

Prepare topping and spread evenly over the bread and bake for 35 to 40 minutes, until puffed and lightly golden.

Serve with "Mama's Maple Syrup".

Mama's Maple Syrup

Mama and Grandmama never used to buy maple syrup at the store. They always made it from scratch. Very simple, and very good.

1 cup sugar
2 tablespoons brown sugar
1/2 cup water
2 teaspoons maple flavoring
1 teaspoon butter flavoring

Boil the sugars and the water for 5 minutes. Remove from heat and add vanilla, maple, and butter flavoring. Pour into a pint jar. Refrigerate leftovers.

Chocolate Sop

When I was in grade school I had a friend who I just loved to go spend the night with because her mother would make us Chocolate Sop for breakfast. Yeah! My Mama did not believe in having chocolate for breakfast, even on Saturdays. So this was a real treat for me. We usually ate it on pancakes or sopped it up with cheese biscuits.

2 tablespoons cocoa	1 1/4 cups sugar
2 tablespoons cornstarch	2 cups milk

In a saucepan mix the cocoa, cornstarch and the sugar together. Put over a medium low heat and slowly add the milk. Cook until thick.

Sweet Potato Waffles

2 large sweet potatoes, baked
2 eggs, separated
2/3 cup sugar
1 1/2 sticks melted butter
2 cups half & half
1 heaping cup of flour

Take the pulp from the sweet potatoes and put into mixing bowl.

Add the 2 egg yolks, sugar, melted butter, half & half and the flour. Mix well.

In a separate bowl beat the egg whites until soft peaks form.

Fold the egg whites into the potato mixture.

Cook in greased waffle iron. The cooking time will depend on your waffle iron.

Breakfast Beignets

(Fried Dough)

Beignet, a fancy word for a big square donut. In New Orleans they may call them beignets but here in Carolina, it's just fried dough. Either way, whatever you choose to call them, they're great. You can make this dough ahead of time and it keeps well in the refrigerator for about a week. Just roll some out in the morning, fry, sprinkle with lots of powdered sugar, grab a cup of coffee, and enjoy.

1 tablespoon active dry yeast
1 1/2 cups warm water
1/2 cup sugar
1 teaspoon salt
2 eggs
1 cup evaporated milk
7 cups all purpose flour, divided
1/4 cup vegetable shortening, melted
oil for frying
powdered sugar in a paper bag

In a large bow, sprinkle yeast over warm water. Stir until dissolved. Add sugar, salt, eggs, and milk and whisk until blended. Add four cups of the flour and beat until smooth. Add shortening and beat in remaining flour. Put in bowl, set in refrigerator overnight.

In the morning roll dough out on floured board to about 1/8 inch thickness. Cut into 2 to 3 inch squares.

Deep fry at medium heat 2 to 3 minutes or until lightly browned on each side.

Put the beignets in the paper bag with the powdered sugar and shake. Serve immediately.

Blueberry Scones

I really like scones because it's more like a biscuit and not as sweet as a muffin. I love the biscuit-like texture too. The scone is certainly not a regular staple on the southern breakfast table, but I think it should be.

2 cups all-purpose flour
1/3 cup sugar
2 tablespoons baking powder
1/3 cup butter
1/2 cup heavy cream
2 eggs beaten (in separate bowls)
1 cup fresh or frozen blueberries
1/4 cup raw sugar

Preheat oven to 357°. Sift together the dry ingredients in a bowl.

Cut the butter into small pieces and blend into the flour mixture with a fork or pastry blender. The mixture should look like coarse crumbs.

Combine the cream and one beaten egg in another bowl, and then add to the flour mixture. Stir in blueberries until just combined and knead gently. Roll or pat the dough on a lightly floured surface cut it into rounds with a cookie cutter.

Put the scones on a baking sheet and brush with the second beaten egg. Sprinkle tops with raw sugar. Bake for approximately 15 minutes or until lightly browned.

Note from Vicki

Raw sugar or Turbinado sugar is made using 100% pure cane sugar from the initial pressing of the cane, which allows the natural molasses to remain in the crystals. It is a golden amber color and provides a great crunch and delicate taste.

Applesauce Pancakes

The applesauce in these pancakes makes a world of difference. My mother used to always make these when we were little.

1 1/2 cups flour
2 teaspoons baking powder
1/2 teaspoon salt
1 tablespoon sugar
1/2 teaspoon cinnamon
2 eggs
1 tablespoon vegetable oil
1 cup milk
1 cup applesauce

In a bowl combine flour, baking powder, salt, sugar and cinnamon.

Beat in the eggs, oil, milk and applesauce until smooth.

Lightly grease a cast iron frying pan or griddle.

Pour batter onto skillet the size that you want your pancakes.

Turn when bubbles start to form on top of pancake and bottom is browned. Serve with butter and maple syrup.

Mama's Sweet Potato Biscuits

2 cups cooked mashed sweet potatoes
1 tablespoon butter
2 cups all purpose flour
1 tablespoon brown sugar
1/2 teaspoon salt
1/4 teaspoon cinnamon
1/4 teaspoon grated nutmeg
1/4 teaspoon baking soda
1/3 cup buttermilk
1 teaspoon fresh lemon juice

Preheat the oven to 375° and grease two baking sheets.

In a large bowl, mix mashed sweet potatoes and butter with the dry ingredients.

Slowly pour in the buttermilk and lemon juice until you have soft dough.

Roll the dough out on a floured surface until it is about 1/2 of an inch thick and cut the biscuits with a biscuit cutter.

Place the biscuits on the baking sheet and bake them for 15 minutes or until they are lightly browned on top.

Serve warm.

The Cinnamon Buns

One year I got a bread making machine for Christmas, and that's when I started making these cinnamon buns. They were a hit from the first time I made them. This is another one of those things that my daughters and niece and nephews ask for. I remember that one night I was making cinnamon buns for the next morning and it was after midnight before I put them in the oven. Well the smell of these buns baking is unbelievable. Before I knew it, the whole family was downstairs eating cinnamons buns at 1:00 AM.

The Dough:
1 cup milk at room temperature
4 tablespoons warm water
1 egg
4 tablespoons melted butter
1/2 of a 3.5 ounce package of vanilla instant pudding
4 cups bread flour
1 tablespoon sugar
1/2 teaspoon salt
1 tablespoon active dry yeast

The Filling:
3/4 cup softened butter
1/2 cup sugar
1/2 cup brown sugar
1 tablespoon cinnamon
1/2 cup chopped pecans (optional)

The Frosting:
1 1/2 cups powdered sugar
4 tablespoons softened butter
1 teaspoon whipping cream
1 teaspoon vanilla

Place the dough ingredients in the bread machine in the order listed and run the machine through the DOUGH cycle.

Remove the dough onto a floured surface and knead lightly.

Roll the dough into a large rectangle.

Spread the butter of the dough and then sprinkle evenly with the other filling ingredients.

Roll the dough into a log and cut into 12 equal pieces.

Place in a prepared 13 x 9 inch baking pan. Cover and place in a warm area to rise. (About an hour).

Preheat oven to 350°.

Bake for 15 to 20 minutes.

Mix all of the frosting ingredients together until smooth.

Spread frosting over warm buns.

Kini Bread

Zucchini Bread is not just a great bread, it becomes a necessity if you put more than one zucchini plant in your garden. This bread freezes really well and is great for breakfast, as a snack or a dessert. By the way, we still call it Kini Bread because that's what my baby girl called it when she was little.

1 cup salad oil
2 cups granulated sugar
2 cups fresh grated zucchini
3 large eggs
1 teaspoon vanilla
3 1/2 cups flour
1 teaspoon salt
1/2 teaspoon baking soda
1/2 teaspoon freshly grated nutmeg
1 teaspoon ground cinnamon
1 cup raisins
1 cup fresh chopped pecans

Preheat oven to 350°.

Mix oil, sugar, and vanilla together in a large bowl. Add the grated zucchini, then the eggs.

In a separate bowl, mix the remaining ingredients together. Then add to zucchini mixture.

Mix well.

Pour into two greased and floured 5x8-inch bread pans.

Bake for 60–70 minutes or until toothpick comes out clean.

Day-Off Blueberry Muffins

Make these muffins when you have sweet, fresh blueberries on hand.

Topping:

1/4 cup chopped pecans	2 tablespoons butter
1/4 cup firmly packed brown sugar	1 tablespoon flour
1/2 cup uncooked regular oats	3/4 cup raw sugar

Muffin Mix:

2 cups all-purpose flour	1 teaspoon vanilla
1/2 cup sugar	3/4 cup buttermilk
2 teaspoons baking powder	1/4 cup oil
1/4 teaspoon baking soda	1 large egg
1/4 teaspoon salt	1 teaspoon lemon zest
1 teaspoon butter flavoring	1 teaspoon lemon juice
2 cups fresh blueberries	

Preheat oven to 400°.

Mix the brown sugar, flour and butter together with a fork until crumbly. Stir in oats and pecans and set aside. DO NOT MIX IN THE RAW SUGAR. Save this for sprinkling on the topping.

Combine 2 cups flour, sugar, baking powder, baking soda and salt in a large bowl.

Whisk together buttermilk, oil, vanilla and butter flavorings, lemon juice and egg; add to flour mixture, stirring just until moistened. Gently fold the blueberries into the batter.

Spoon batter into greased muffin pans, filling two-thirds full and sprinkle batter with topping. Sprinkle topping with raw sugar.

Bake for 15 to 20 minutes or until golden brown.

Potato Crusted Quiche

3 cups frozen shredded potatoes
5 tablespoons melted butter
1 cup finely chopped cooked ham or sausage
1 cup shredded sharp cheese
1/2 cup finely chopped onions
1/2 cup finely chopped green peppers
3 eggs
1/2 cup milk or cream
1/2 teaspoon salt
1/2 teaspoon pepper

Pour ½ of the melted butter into the bottom of a 9 inch pie pate.

Press all of the liquid you can out of the potatoes, pat with a paper towel or clean kitchen towel to dry and press them into bottom and up the sides of the plate and drizzle the remaining butter on the top.

Bake at 425° for 25 minutes or until golden brown. Remove from oven.

In the potato crust layer the ham, onion, green pepper, and the cheese.

In a separate bowl mix the eggs with the milk and salt and pepper. Pour the egg mixture over the cheese.

Bake at 375° for 35-40 minutes or until set.

Vicki's East Coast Breakfast

This is the ultimate breakfast for seafood lovers. What a way to start your day off, with sweet crabmeat and delectable shrimp. This will impress your favorite guests for that special breakfast or for brunch, dinner or supper too.

6 English muffins
1 stick of butter
1 pound of crabmeat
1/2 pound of boiled shrimp
6 eggs
1 tablespoon vinegar
Hollandaise Sauce

Split the English muffins and toast until golden.

In a large skillet melt the butter and add the crabmeat and shrimp. Cook just enough to warm through.

Prepare Hollandaise Sauce (see recipe)

In another skillet bring 2 cups of water and the vinegar to a slow simmer. Break each egg into a saucer and gently slide into the water. Cook until the desired doneness.

Assembly:

1. Take an English muffin and put on a plate.

2. Put a very large spoonful of the crabmeat/shrimp mixture on top of the muffin. (overflowing).

3. Top with other half of muffin.

4. Remove egg from water and set on a paper towel to absorb all of the water, then place on top of muffin.

5. Pour Hollandaise generously over the top

6. Sprinkle with fresh chopped parsley

"Grandma's Aprons"

If you grew up in the south chances are most of the women that lived in your neighborhood wore aprons, and not just when they cooked, they wore them all day long. So what has happened to them? Where did they go?

All of my Grandmama's wore aprons. As a matter of fact, the only time in my life that I saw my great-grandmother, Mammy, without an apron on, was at my wedding. They all made their own aprons too, and they didn't look like those fancy kinds of chefs apron's that are around today. Nope, most were made out of printed cotton, just a skirted apron that tied around the waist, and most of the time with a pocket. They used material that was left over from making a dress, a quilt or even flour and sugar sacks.

So what are they good for, why did they wear them? We should really revive them. Aprons are very useful and are great for loads of things, not to mention hiding that stomach pooch. You know they didn't have paper towels back then!! Can you imagine life without paper towels??!!

That's the first thing a woman did in the morning, pick out an apron. In the house her apron was used for taking things out of the oven, wiping up little spills, drying your hands and dusting off a table when you see the neighbor coming up in the yard. Now if you had your kids or grandkids running around an apron was used for wiping little hands, getting the dirt off of that skinned knee before you put the mercurochrome on it, and of course that classic of spitting on the corner of the apron and getting little faces clean. They also used them outside for countless things. Let's say you are outside hosing down the flowers and get your hands wet, you just use your apron to wipe them dry … and while you're out there you notice in the garden that you've got some tomatoes and peppers that need picking, so gather them up the apron corners and load up the bounty.

Later on you go to feed the chickens (doubled duty this time). You gather up those apron corners, fill it with corn and scratch and throw it out to the chickens and while the chicks are busy eating you make your way to the coop and again gather those apron corners and collect the eggs.

Hey you *Sweet Tea Girls,* how about making a revival. Bring back the apron!! Today we could coordinate them with our jeans and tops, put a little pocket for our cell phone, a little mirror on the apron tie, one corner could be like a damp wet nap, a place for some sticky notes and a pen (I can't live without sticky notes) … hey this could go on and on … Maybe I should call Dolce & Gabbana and see if they're interested.

Vegetables
&
Side Dishes

As my Daddy
used to say, the **"with it".**

Vegetable stand in Arapahoe, North Carolina

"We don't need a melting pot in this country, folks. We need a salad bowl. In a salad bowl, you put in the different things. You want the vegetables—the lettuce, the cucumbers, the onions, the green peppers—to maintain their identity. You appreciate the differences."

—Jane Elliot

"Collards"

Most of the older folks around will tell you not to eat collards until after the first frost has fallen because it makes them sweeter and more tender. It would not be Thanksgiving or Christmas in the south without a mess of collards at the table. Of course in our family we ate collards all through the year and they all tasted good to me. I think the biggest secret to good collards is the meat you cook them in. My Grandma Lotha used to always cook her collards with corned ham or with pig tails and my Grandma Velma usually used fat back or ham hocks. Either way is great but distinctly different, you will have two very different tastes for your collards. The collards will take on the flavor of the meat. Collards without meat?.... Are you crazy?

I loved to watch Grandma Velma take up her collards. To begin with, she never cut up her collards before cooking. She cooked the leaves whole. After they were cooked the first thing she would do was take out the potatoes and dumplings and arrange them neatly on a plate. She made sure that there were no little bits of collard leaf stuck to any of them. Then she would take out the meat and put it in a bowl. If it was a ham hock she would cut the tender meat off of the bone making it easy to serve. Now for the collards. She would drain off all of the liquid into a bowl and then take a dinner plate and put it on top of the collards to help push out all of the excess pot liquor. When she was satisfied she had gotten enough of the liquid out she would put the collards in a bowl and get her big knife and fork and chop them up (no fancy chopping utensils for her). When they were chopped to her satisfaction she would go back to the pot liquor she had saved, take a spoon, get some of the fat from the top and drizzle it over the collards. That was her ritual and I've seen her do it a million times. Of course I try to imitate her, but somehow it just doesn't turn out the same and then again maybe it's only in my mind that its not the same, because I just want my Grandma to be there doing it.

First Frost Collards with Potatoes & Cornmeal Dumplings

5 to 6 pounds fresh collards
About 4 slices fat back
1 or 2 ham hocks or about a pound of corned pig tails
Water
6 to 8 potatoes peeled and cut in half
1 teaspoon sugar
Salt and Pepper to taste

In a large pot fry the fatback until golden brown. Score the ham hock with a knife (or pig tails) and put into pot with enough water to cover. Bring to a boil and then simmer for about an hour. Wash collards and cut out any big stems. Roll up collard leaves and cut diagonally about an inch thick. Add the collards and cook about 30 minutes. Add potatoes and corn meal dumplings. (Make sure they are down in the liquid). Cook until done, about another 20 minutes. Drain off the liquid and add the sugar, salt and pepper. Stir well and serve.

Corn Meal Dumplings

Corn meal dumplings are something most southerners grew up on. We put them in collards, cabbage, green beans and butter beans, beef stew and crab stew. Cornmeal has always been abundant in the south

1 cup of corn meal (not self rising)   Water

2 tablespoons of AP flour   Salt & pepper

Mix together the meal and four with enough water to make a firm ball. Season with salt and pepper. Make into patties (1 and 1/2 inch circles and about 1/2 in thick) and add to cooking broth. Cook for approximately 15 minutes.

Company Scalloped Potatoes

8 to 10 medium potatoes peeled and sliced
1/4 cup finely minced onion
1/2 cup parmesan cheese
3/4 cup parsley
2 teaspoons salt
1/2 teaspoon pepper
1 can of cream of mushroom soup
1 cup milk

Preheat oven to 350°.

Grease a 9 x 13 baking pan.

Layer the potatoes, onion, cheese, parsley and salt and pepper into 3 layers in the baking pan.

Mix the soup and milk together and pour over the potatoes.

Bake covered tightly for 1 hour.

Remove foil and bake uncovered for 30 more minutes.

Aunt Hazel's Squash Casserole

My Aunt Hazel, my Grandmama Velma's sister, was a really good cook. She just didn't like to cook. To tell the truth, she refused to cook. But she did break down and cook this squash casserole for several get togethers when she was forced to bring something. One of her favorites, and mine too.

2 pounds yellow crookneck squash, chopped
2 small onions, chopped
1/2 stick butter
1/4 cup vegetable oil
1 can cream of chicken soup
1 pint sour cream
1 can water chestnuts, chopped
3 cups Cheddar cheese, grated
1 package cornbread dressing mix
1 stick butter, melted

Preheat oven to 350°.

Melt ½ stick butter and ¼ cup oil in frying pan and cook squash and onions until tender.

Add soup, sour cream, and water chestnuts; set aside.

Mix melted butter and dressing mix and line casserole dish with half of the dressing mix. Sprinkle small portion of cheese over dressing mix.

Pour in squash mixture. Sprinkle remaining cheese over squash and top with remaining dressing mix.

Bake 30 to 40 minutes.

Squash and Onions

Everyone that grows up in the south knows that 2 squash plants will feed a whole neighborhood. Nevertheless, we always planted a lot of squash and this dish is a staple during the summer, usually served several (or more) times a week.

2 tablespoons of bacon grease (olive oil if you must)
5 or 6 crookneck yellow squash
1 large onion
Salt and pepper

Wash the squash and trim off the ends. Then cut into about 1/2 inch chunks (not slices).

Chop up the onion.

Heat up the fat in a cast iron skillet and add the squash and onions.

Keep the heat on medium high to high. Do not cover.

You don't want to steam them.

Cook for about 10 minutes.

You want to be able to get some brown color on the onions and squash.

Southerners can't stand to eat alone. If we're going to cook a mess of greens we want to eat them with a mess of people."

—Julia Reed

Real Deal Mac and Cheese

This is a must at all of our family gatherings.

16 ounces elbow macaroni
2 quarts boiling water
2 teaspoons salt
1 stick butter
1/2 cup flour
1 cup evaporated milk
4 cups whole milk
1 teaspoon salt
2 teaspoons prepared mustard
8 ounces of cream cheese
4 cups sharp cheese, grated
1 sleeve of buttery crackers, crushed
1/2 stick melted butter

Preheat oven to 375°.

In a large pot bring the water and 2 teaspoons of salt to a boil. Pour in the macaroni and cook for 4 (four) minutes. Drain and pour macaroni in a well greased 9x13 casserole.

In a large saucepan melt the butter, stir in the flour and cook for 1 minute over medium heat. Slowly add the milk and continue to cook over medium heat, stirring often, until sauce comes to a boil and thickens. Remove from heat and stir in the salt, mustard and grated cheese, until cheese is melted.

Mix together the macaroni and cheese sauce and pour into a buttered casserole.

Mix the crushed crackers with the melted butter and spread over the top of the macaroni. Bake for 25 to 30 minutes.

Mama's Fried Apples

My mama loves apples. She takes a trip to the North Carolina mountain's almost every year and always brings back a couple of bushels of apples with her. This is a great side dish with just about anything. You can serve it over some vanilla ice cream for a dessert!

6 large apples (about 6 cups, sliced)
1/4 cup butter
1/4 sugar
1/4 cup brown sugar
1 teaspoon red hot cinnamon candies

Peel and slice apples into thick slices. Place into a medium size skillet with butter.

Cook over medium heat until just tender.

Stir in the sugar(s) and the cinnamon candies and cover the skillet. Cook another 5 minutes or until brown sugar and candies are dissolved and thick.

Grilled Corn

When fresh sweet corn is at its peak this is one of my favorite ways to eat it. All of the fresh flavor of the corn stays in when cooked this way.

6 ears of fresh sweet corn with husks left on

Soak the corn in water for at least 30 minutes

Place the corn on the grill, medium heat turning frequently.

When the shucks are no longer green the corn is done.

Remove the shucks and the silks

Drench in sweet butter

Easy Corn Soufflé

1 16 ounce can of cream style corn
2 10 ounce cans of whole kernel corn
1 cup of sour cream
1 stick of butter at room temperature
1 8.5 ounce package of corn muffin mix
1 cup of sharp cheddar cheese grated

Preheat oven to 350° and grease a 1 ½ quart casserole dish.

Mix all of the corn, sour cream, butter and corn muffin mix together until it is a smooth consistency. Pour this mixture into the casserole dish. Sprinkle the grated cheese over the top and bake for 50 to 60 minutes.

Rice and Tomatoes

This is my comfort food. Super simple, but oh so good.

1 cup rice
2 cups water
1/2 teaspoon salt
1/2 teaspoon pepper
1 can diced tomatoes (or if you canned some from your garden that's even better)

Put the rice, water and salt in a lidded saucepan and bring to a boil. Reduce the heat to low and cook until the rice is done. Add the can of tomatoes and heat through. That's it. I told you it was simple.

Scalloped Tomatoes

1 28 ounce can of tomatoes
1 small onion finely diced
1/4 cup of butter
1 1/2 cups bread cut into cubes
1/2 cup brown sugar
Salt and pepper

Preheat oven to 350°.

Sauté the onion in the butter in a medium saucepan.

Add the bread cubes and sugar and cook slowly for about 5 minutes. Add the tomatoes and the seasonings.

Place this mixture in a buttered casserole dish.

Bake for 45 minutes.

Fresh Speckled Butter Beans (Backer Beans)

I can remember many days setting in Grandma Velma's porch swing shelling butter beans and swatting mosquitoes and yellow flies. She always had a big garden so she was always picking beans, shelling beans or snapping beans. It seems like this dish was one that always graced her table. We always had these on days that we were taking in tobacco hence the name "Backer Beans"

About 2 quarts water
1 ham hock
6 cups (about 2 pounds) fresh shelled speckled butter beans
Salt and pepper
5 potatoes peeled and quartered
6 to 8 pods fresh okra (leave whole)
(You can also put in some corn meal dumplin's)

In a large pan, bring the water and ham hock to a boil.

Simmer for 30 minutes, to season the water.

Add the beans and bring the water back to a boil, then turn down the heat and simmer, partially covered, for 30 minutes.

Season with salt and pepper (the amounts will depend on the saltiness of your meat).

Add the potatoes and lay the whole okra on top

Cook another 30 minutes or until the beans are tender and creamy inside.

Remove ham hock, potatoes and okra and place on serving dish. Serve along side beans.

Roasted Asparagus

Fresh asparagus (about 1 pound)
2 tablespoons olive oil
1 teaspoon kosher salt
1 teaspoon freshly ground black pepper
1/2 cup freshly grated Parmesan
1/2 lemon

Preheat the oven to 400°.

Hold the asparagus stalk in both hands, bend the asparagus and it will break at the spot where the tough part ends. Lay them in a single layer on a sheet pan and drizzle with olive oil and sprinkle with salt and pepper. Roast for about 10 minutes, until tender. Sprinkle with the Parmesan and return to the oven for another minute. Squeeze lemon over asparagus.

Candied Sweet Potatoes

My Grandma Lotha always made these and they were the best! The potatoes will be firm, soft in the middle with a sticky sweet glaze. They will get a little color but be careful not to burn them. I use a heavy cast iron skillet but you can also use a non stick frying pan.

1/2 cup butter	2 cups sugar
6 to 7 sweet potatoes peeled and sliced	Dash of salt
1/2 teaspoon of cinnamon	
1/4 teaspoon of fresh grated nutmeg	

Melt butter in a large skillet over medium-low heat. In bowl combine sugar, cinnamon, nutmeg and salt. Add sliced potatoes to melted butter, coat all potatoes with butter. Sprinkle sugar mixture over potatoes, stir. Cover and reduce heat to low. Stirring occasionally, Cook for 50-60 minutes, or until potatoes are tender.

New Year's Day
Black-Eyed Peas

It doesn't matter if you like black eyed peas or not, on New Year's Day you have to eat a bowl full. The black eyed peas will bring you good luck during the upcoming year. To go along with that you have to eat some greens, which down here means collard greens. The greens will take care of your money problems for the year.

1 pound dry black-eyed peas
2 quarts water (If you cooked a picnic on top of the stove use the water you cooked it in for the beans)
2 cups cooked ham in pieces
Salt and pepper to taste
2 medium onions, diced

Wash peas and put in a large pot. Add enough water to fill pot 3/4 full. Stir in ham and diced onions, and season with salt and pepper. Bring to a boil. Cover the pot, and simmer on low heat for 2 to 3 hours, or until the peas are tender.

Baked Sweet Potatoes

Did you ever walk into a house filled with the smell of baking sweet potatoes? That aroma will automatically bring a smile to your face. Sweet Potatoes are definitely a southern staple. Every year my Daddy would go out and buy a bushel or two of sweet potatoes and how we had them most often, was baked. Sometimes we tend to forget that some of the simplest things are the best.

6 sweet potatoes (try to get them all about the same size)
Crisco

Wash the sweet potatoes and dry well.

Rub Crisco liberally all over each of the potatoes.

You can wrap each potato in foil if you like (I don't). If you don't wrap them make sure to put a layer of foil on your baking sheet as the natural sugars are going to ease out.

Bake at 375° for about an hour depending on the size of the potatoes.

When done either peel, cut in half and serve or leave unpeeled and split down the middle and load it up with butter. It's the best.

Real Mashed Potatoes

I hope that everyone already knows how to make mashed potatoes. When I started to work on this book my daughter Kristen was going through some of my recipes and she said "Mama you don't have mashed potatoes in here!" Well mashed potatoes just happen to be her all time favorite food. I told her that I was sure most people already knew how to make mashed potatoes but she insisted so here is my mashed potato recipe.

These are just regular old everyday mashed potatoes like your grandma made, no garlic added, no green onions, no horseradish.

8 to 10 medium potatoes cut into chunks
Cold water to cover plus 2 teaspoons of salt
1 stick of butter
1/2 cup of Sour Cream
2 teaspoons of salt
Whole Milk

In a large pot put in the cold water and the potatoes and salt. Cook the potatoes over a medium high heat until soft (not mushy. Drain potatoes.

Put back in the pot and add the butter and salt. Whip with mixer until there are no lumps.

Add the milk a little at a time until the potatoes are at the consistency you desire (don't use too much.)

Note from Vicki

You know sometimes you will see a bag of potatoes at the store that have a greenish tint. Don't buy them.

Sweet Potato Fluff

This is always served at any special gathering we have at my house. You can almost say it's a dessert it's so good. Pecans with sweet potatoes is a great combination.

Bake enough sweet potatoes in the oven to make 3 cups of mashed potatoes (Rub potatoes with Crisco™ and bake at 375° for 1 hour or until potatoes are soft.)
1 cup sugar
2 eggs
1/3 stick of melted butter
1/2 teaspoon salt
1 cup canned evaporated milk
1 teaspoon vanilla extract
1 teaspoon butter flavoring

Topping:
1/3 cup softened butter
1/3 cup all-purpose flour
1 cup brown sugar
1 cup chopped pecans

Preheat oven to 350°.

With a hand or stand mixer mix the potatoes until no lumps appear. Add the sugar, salt and eggs. Mix well. Pour in the butter, milk and flavorings. Mix well and pour into a greased baking dish.

Bake for 30 minutes and then remove from oven.

Mix the topping ingredients together and sprinkle over the potato mixture.

Return to oven and cook for an additional 20 minutes.

The Best Baked Beans

2 21 ounce cans pork and beans
6 slices bacon
2 cloves minced garlic
3/4 cup chopped onion
1/2 cup chopped green pepper
1/2 cup catsup
1/3 cup molasses
1/3 cup brown sugar
1 tablespoon mustard

Preheat oven to 350°.

Fry bacon, remove from pan and set aside.

Sauté the onion, garlic and green pepper in the bacon grease.

In a greased baking dish combine the sautéed ingredients with the beans and the other remaining ingredients.

Bake for 1 hour.

Remove from oven and crumble the cooked bacon over the top.

"Listen to me, and listen to me good."

—Dick Banks (Daddy)

Dilled Green Beans

I got this recipe from a friend of mine who attended culinary school. Now it's my all time favorite way to fix green beans.

1 pound fresh tipped and tailed green beans or a 1 pound bag of frozen green beans
1 tablespoon butter
1 cup fresh sliced mushrooms
6 slices bacon
1 can sliced water chestnuts
1 tablespoon soy sauce
1 tablespoon fresh dill weed, chopped

If you are using fresh green beans *blanch them in salted boiling water for 3 minutes. Set aside.

In a large frying pan melt the butter and add the mushrooms. Cook over a medium high heat until mushrooms are nicely browned. Remove from pan and set aside.

Add the bacon to the pan and cook until crispy. Remove from pan and set aside.

Leave the bacon drippings in the pan and add your green beans. Turn the heat to high. You want to cook all of the water out of the beans and have them start to brown a little. When beans have reached this stage add in the soy sauce and water chestnuts. Cook for 2 minutes more. Remove from heat and stir in crumbled bacon, mushrooms and dill weed. Serve while hot.

Note from Vicki

To *Blanch* means to submerge the vegetable into boiling water, removed after a brief interval (depending on the vegetable usually 1 to 3 minutes) and then submerge into iced water or placed under cold running water (shocked) to halt the cooking process.

Southern Style String Beans

My Grandma always had string beans in her garden. I loved to pick them and I loved to eat them. You can use flat beans for this recipe too.

2 pounds fresh green beans
4 slices bacon, diced
3/4 cup diced salt pork (fatback)
2 cans chicken stock
8 to 10 new potatoes
Salt and pepper

Tip, tail and string the green beans and cut into one inch pieces.

In a cast iron dutch oven, or heavy pot, cook the bacon and salt pork over medium heat until the fat is rendered.

Put in the chicken stock and green beans. Cover with water, bring to a boil, then turn to low heat and cook for 30 minutes.

Add the new potatoes to the pot, taste for seasoning and add salt and pepper. Cook for an additional 30 minutes on low heat. Add more water if necessary. These beans will be "fall apart" tender. Serve with cornbread.

Note from Vicki

To *Tip, Tail and String* the beans means to snap the end off of each end of the bean and normally a "string" will be attached to one of the ends along the "seam" of the bean, pull the string off.

"Gospel and Honky Tonk"

Music has always been a part of my life ever since I can remember. The music came from my Daddy's side of the family. My Mama said the only thing her family could play was the radio. My Granddaddy and my Daddy both played the guitar and sang, and my aunt played the piano and sang. I guess I grew up thinking everybody could sing and I didn't understand it when someone said they couldn't. I thought it was something everyone could do. I started singing probably as soon as I started talking.

Daddy, "Saturday Night" Singing

When my Granddaddy Mack would come over he would always tell me, "Go get that guitar girl and let me show you how to play." He had this finger picking style of playing that I loved, but never have been quite able to duplicate. He only sang two songs as far as I can remember. "Send Me the Pillow that you Dream On" and "Faded Rose." He was quite a character, my Granddaddy Mack, and he always made me smile. A gentle soul who liked to have a good time. Every time I get a whiff of a combination of Vitalis Hair Tonic, Camel cigarettes and Schlitz beer, I think of him.

My Daddy was always playing the guitar and singing. Back in the 60's he and a friend headed out for Nashville, trying to make it big. The closest they came to hitting the big time there was seeing Roy Acuff in a local diner. They did go up and talk to Mr. Acuff (we never have been a shy bunch), but all he was interested in at the time was getting some good meatloaf for his lunch. Daddy told me they ran out of the little money they had early on, and I remember them telling stories of going into restaurants and just ordering coffee. Back then instead of those little creamer packets they give you today, they would give you a little pitcher of cream. Well they only ordered 2 cups of coffee, but the waitress had to bring them 4 pitchers of cream. Daddy said the wise waitress kind of gave him a sly smile saying, "You boys sure do like a lot of cream in your coffee."

Leaving Nashville behind, they came home and sang in Honky Tonks on Saturday night and churches on Sunday morning. Now there's not a thing wrong with that. I've been told by many a preacher that the Lord does love country music.

I guess I started singing for people, other than my family, when I was about seven years old. Sometimes I would get to go to the Honky Tonks and sing a song or two before it got too late. The first songs I ever sang in public were "Your Cheatin' Heart" and "Once a Day", but of course I was singing in church before I can remember singing in church.

My Daddy had tons of country albums and I listened to them over and over again. If you played Merle Haggard's "Branded Man" album for me today, or Loretta Lynn's "Coal Miner's Daughter" album, I guarantee you that I know just about every word to every song. Country music was just as much a part of me as eating and sleeping.

I recall singing at a big square dance one time, I guess I was about ten, and belted out Tammy Wynette's newest release, D-I-V-O-R-C-E. I remember people stopping what they were doing and turning around to look at me, and I remember my Daddy smiling and shaking his head as he stood beside me playing along and joining in on the chorus. I guess it was kind of a hoot, a ten year old girl singing about her kids and divorce. We had lots of special times singing together through the years.

In the early 70's me and my Daddy, and that same Nashville bound friend from the 60's trip, started singing in different churches pretty much every Sunday. One of the best things was that most of the time, the churches would always have a dinner since they were having special singing. That is by far some of the best food around and not only did we look forward to singing on Sunday's, but we always knew we were in for a great meal.

"Sunday Morning Singing "Rodney Ensley, Daddy
(Dick Banks), and Mr. White Ensley.

Later on after I got married, we were still singing, going from church to church, and my husband, Bobby, would go along most of the time. Even though he can't carry a tune in a bucket, he was good at carrying amplifiers, guitars and microphones. There was a church in a little town called Whortonsville where we used to sing quite often. Well you could bet your last dollar Bobby was going to make sure he was along on that day. These people really knew how to cook. Fried shrimp and soft shell crabs were always on the table along with the best desserts and "with it" you've ever had. He never missed a singing at Whortonsville.

I recall one Saturday night the Whortonsville church was having a sing. We performed in the sanctuary and after a couple of hours of singing songs about Jonah and the Whale, Lazarus and old standards like "Where No One Stands Alone", "How Great Thou Art" and "On The Wings of a Dove", we stopped to go out back to the fellowship building and eat. Well some of the folks still wanted to hear some music so we brought the guitars back there, pulled up some stools and my crazy Daddy breaks out singing, "Oh Lord it's hard to be humble when you're perfect in every way. I can't wait to look in the mirror 'cause I get better looking each day. To know me is to love me I must be a heck of a man. Oh Lord it's hard to be humble but I'm doing the best that I can." They still let us eat.... and even invited us back the next week-end!

"Country Stores"

No, we didn't have a Food Lion or Harris Teeter or even a Piggly Wiggly. We just had the community store. They were all about the same, a one room building with a counter. Some of the stores might have a cooler for meat and some just had a chest type deep freezer.

Within about a 3 mile radius of where I lived there were five stores. Mr. Johnny Parson's Store, Miss Sina Scott's Store, Miss Bertie Hall's Market, Mr. Jug Lindsay's Store, and Mr. Lionel Willis' Grocery.

I always went with my Grandma Velma and Granddaddy Alton on Friday nights to Mr. Johnny Parson's store. They only bought things like flour and sugar and of course hoop cheese. Sometimes they would buy chicken and maybe some beef if there was something special coming up. All of the vegetables came from their garden so they never bought any vegetable except maybe lettuce, and they killed their own pigs so they didn't buy any pork products either. Of course granddaddy had to buy his short, no-filter Camel™ cigarettes. And forget about buying soft drinks (drinks as we called them). The only time you got that treat was when you were working in tobacco. At meal time you drank sweet tea, water or milk, no other choices available.

I really liked Miss Sina's store because she had a big potbelly stove in the middle of the store with rocking chairs around it. Every time you went in those chairs were always filled with some of the local folks telling stories. She had a deep freeze that she kept her ice cream in and I always got a creamsicle when I went there or a pack of nabs (you only got 4 then) and a small co-cola. (We always said co-cola not Coke or Coca-Cola. Even when we meant a Pepsi it was still a co-cola). If I was with my mama I had to get cup ice cream because she didn't want me getting my clothes messed up with dripping ice cream, but that was okay because there was something I loved about getting those little wooden spoons to eat the ice cream with. After I finished eating my ice cream I would keep that little sliver of a piece of wood for weeks.

The next down the line was Mr. Jug Lindsay's store. It was near the curve at the end of Goose Creek Road. My Daddy stopped by there some to get his Pall Malls and I would sometimes get some penny candy there.

Miss Birdie's was our choice for ice cream. She would scoop it out and put it in a cone for you. One, two or three scoops, but you had better not take too long deciding which kind you wanted because she didn't seem to have a lot of patience with indecision. My favorite was the chocolate revel. I remember one time I went in and asked for a cone and she asked me pretty sternly what kind I wanted. She just about scared me to death and I told her I wanted chocolate revel with a lot of revel in it. She just laughed at me and shook her head.

My Granddaddy Mack also used to take me out to Miss Bertie after he got home from work and buy me silvertips (We now call them Hershey's Kisses) but they will always be silver tips to me.

Mr. Lionel had a bigger store with isles and a meat counter in the back and Mr. Lionel was always there talking up a storm to everybody. I would go to his store with my Grandma Lotha or Aunt Bunny.

I miss those stores. It was fun going shopping and stopping in to get ice cream was a real treat. They always knew your name, almost like family. Somehow going to buy groceries at the Food Lion just isn't as much fun.

Salads
&
Soups

Another day of fun on the creek with family and friends.

It's difficult to think anything but pleasant thoughts while eating a home-grown tomato.

—Lewis Grizzard

"Milk from the Store?"

We didn't buy milk from the store until I was well into my teens, and when we did have to face the fact that Granddaddy had sold his cow, and there was no more milk from Bessie, well, I didn't like it. When you're used to drinking "real" milk that milk in the paper cartons just didn't taste right to me.

We lived on a dirt road right down from my Granddaddy and Grandmama's house. It was my job to make sure we always had enough milk at our house. Of course I was over there everyday anyway. It wasn't like it was a real chore. I loved to watch Grandmama pour the milk from the milking pail and strain it through cheesecloth into a big white enamel pan with a red rim. Then she would put it in the refrigerator to cool down.

My favorite part was when she would take a spoon and skim the thick layer of cream off of the top and put it in a jar. I would beg her to let me do it, but she said that I would get too much milk in with it, so I had to be satisfied with watching her. I'd bring over the big glass half-gallon orange juice jars (yes orange juice came in jars back then) and she would pour the creamy milk into the jar right from the pan without spilling a drop.

Sometimes she would let me help her make some butter. We would take the cream and some salt and put it in a small churn that she had, and I would turn the handle until it got thick. She had a wooden butter mold and she would let me scoop the butter into it. When it came out of the refrigerator the next day, and out of the mold, it had a pretty star design on the top. As for the cream.... Believe me it is probably a good thing that I don't know someone who has a cow where I can get that cream from again. I ate it almost every day. I can't even begin to tell you how good thick cow's cream was on Grandmama's homemade grape preserves and a hot biscuit. Oh Lord, I'm in heaven.

Down South Potato Salad

6 large potatoes
2 eggs hard-boiled and mashed
1 stalk celery, chopped very fine
1/2 cup sweet pickle cubes (not pickle relish)
1 tablespoon prepared mustard
1/2 to 1 cup of mayonnaise
Salt and pepper
Fresh chopped parsley for garnish
Paprika for sprinkling

Peel potatoes and chop into small cubes. Place potatoes in pot of boiling water and cook until tender but still firm, about 15 minutes; drain.

In a large bowl, combine the potatoes, eggs, pickle cubes, mustard, mayo and salt and pepper. Gently mix together and serve warm.

Sprinkle top of potato salad with Paprika, garnish with parsley.

Note from Vicki

I make two kinds of potato salad. One is the "Southern Style" which is above and the other is, well, "The Other" Potato Salad. I would never put onions in the Southern Style, but I love the onions in the "The Other". They are two totally different salads but both very good.

The Other Potato Salad

6 to 8 large potatoes
1 medium red onion finely diced
1/2 cup fresh chopped parsley
1 tablespoon fresh chopped dill
3/4 cup sour cream
3/4 cup mayonnaise
2 teaspoons vinegar
1 tablespoon sugar

Peel potatoes and chop into cubes. Place potatoes in pot of cold water and cook until tender but still firm, about 15 minutes. Drain the potatoes and immediately add the onion while the potatoes are still hot (doing this cooks the onion just enough to get rid of the raw taste). Mix the sour cream, mayonnaise, vinegar and sugar together and pour over the potatoes. Add in the herbs and salt and pepper. Mix well. Can either be served at room temperature or chilled.

Tomato and Basil Salad

My northern friends refer to this as Caprese. Sometimes instead of slicing the tomatoes and the cheese I will dice them and mix all of the ingredients together. I think I might like it better that way.... you decide.

3 or 4 ripe tomatoes sliced thickly
A handful of fresh basil
Fresh (soft) Buffalo Mozzarella Cheese (sliced)
Salt & Pepper
Good Extra Virgin Olive Oil

Layer tomato, basil and cheese in a circle.

Sprinkle with salt and pepper, drizzle with olive oil.

Spinach and Orange Salad

6 to 8 cups of fresh spinach
1/4 cup sliced toasted almonds
2 tablespoons chopped green onions (or purple onion)
3/4 cup sliced fresh mushrooms
3/4 cup of orange sections or 1 can of mandarin oranges drained

Dressing:
1/4 cup vegetable oil
1 teaspoon sesame oil
2 tablespoons sugar
2 tablespoons vinegar
1 tablespoon fresh parsley
1/2 teaspoon salt
1/4 teaspoon pepper
Dash of hot sauce

Combine all dressing ingredients in a jar and shake well.

Chill the dressing and pour over just before serving.

Southport Cole Slaw

The first time I had this was at a friend's house in Southport. I thought, "What in the world is she making with those Ramen Noodles?" I can tell you, I was hesitant to eat it at first. It just didn't sound like it would taste good at all. Boy was I wrong.

2 3 ounce packages of Oriental Flavor Ramen Noodles
1 pound of fresh shredded cabbage
1 cup of slivered almonds
1/2 cup sunflower seeds
1 bunch of green onions, chopped

Dressing:
3/4 cup vegetable oil
1/2 cup cider vinegar
4 tablespoons sugar
Soup seasoning packets

Combine the cabbage, almonds, sunflower seeds and onion. Add the dressing and toss together. Refrigerate this for at least an hour.

Break the Ramen Noodles into small pieces and just before serving, toss them into the slaw mixture.

Quick Coleslaw

You can make up a batch of coleslaw in no time at all with those new bags of shredded cabbage and carrots. I've been making slaw this way since I was about twelve. I've never bought any coleslaw dressing, this is so easy.

Note from Vicki

The portion amounts here are tricky so I am not going to give them to you.... That's what cooking is all about anyway.... You make it to your taste. So I've given you all of the ingredients. Get started.

Shredded cabbage and carrots or coleslaw mix
Sweet pickle cubes
Mayonnaise
Vinegar
Sugar
Salt and pepper

The exact amounts are up to YOU.
Start with ABOUT a cup of mayonnaise.
Add ABOUT ½ to ¾ cup of sweet pickle cubes. (This does not mean sweet pickle relish!)
Add ABOUT 1 or 2 tablespoons of vinegar (apple cider vinegar)
Add ABOUT 1 or 2 tablespoons of sugar

Mix and taste and add a little at a time to get exactly what you like.

Sprinkle the cabbage with salt & pepper and add your sauce a little at a time until you get the desired consistency.

Cucumbers, Onion & Tomato Salad

Some form of fresh from the garden cucumbers and tomatoes are always on the dinner table during the summer months in a southern household. I never even really thought about putting a recipe for something like this in a book ... I just thought it was something that everyone did until someone was visiting when I served this and just raved about it. Who knew?

3 cucumbers, peeled and very thinly sliced
1 small onion, thinly sliced and broken apart
2 medium tomatoes peeled and diced
2 teaspoons sugar
Salt and pepper
Cider Vinegar
Olive Oil

Combine all vegetables.
Sprinkle with the sugar, salt & pepper
Add enough cider vinegar to cover about half way and then drizzle about ¼ cup or less of olive oil over them.
Mix well and chill.

Note from Vicki

About cucumbers. If I don't have fresh from the garden cukes, I always buy the long cucumbers that are wrapped. I think they call them English Cucumbers. Anyway, you won't believe how long those cucumbers will last in the refrigerator! When others have turned to mush these are still nice and firm. Yes, they are more expensive, but they last so long you never ever have any waste.

"Farming looks mighty easy when your plow is a pencil, and you're a thousand miles from the corn field."

—Dwight D. Eisenhower

Key West Spinach Salad

The first time I ever ate a spinach salad was on our honeymoon in Key West, Florida. I loved it from that moment on. Every time I make Spinach Salad for Bobby we always end up talking about the fun we had in Key West. Great memories, great salad.

1 pound fresh spinach
3/4 cup of sliced fresh mushrooms
2 hard-cooked eggs, chopped
2 tablespoons cider vinegar
1/4 cup olive oil
Pinch of sugar
Salt and pepper
10 slices bacon

Wash and trim spinach; pat dry with paper towels.

Sprinkle over the top of the greens the chopped boiled eggs and the mushrooms.

Fry bacon until crisp; drain and reserve drippings. Crumble the bacon and sprinkle over the greens.

Prepare Dressing:
Combine vinegar, oil, bacon drippings, sugar, salt, and pepper. Mix well.

Pour dressing over the spinach mixture.

Serve immediately.

Homecoming Layered Salad

3 cups chopped romaine or iceberg lettuce
3 cups baby spinach
Salt and pepper
6 hard-cooked eggs, sliced
1 can sliced water chestnuts
2 cups fresh broccoli cut into small bite size pieces
2 cups frozen peas, thawed
1 pound bacon, crisp-cooked, drained, and crumbled
2 cups (8 ounces) shredded mild Cheddar cheese
1 cup mayonnaise
1 cup sour cream
2 tablespoons sugar
1 tablespoon cider vinegar
1/4 cup sliced green onion with tops

In a large salad bowl of 13 x 9 dish begin layering.

1st layer the lettuce sprinkle with salt and pepper.
2nd layer the spinach
3rd layer the sliced boiled eggs and sprinkle with salt and pepper
4th water chestnuts
5th broccoli
6th peas
7th bacon
8th cheese
9th Combine mayonnaise, sour cream vinegar and sugar and spread over the top.
10th chopped green onions

Cover and chill 24 hours or overnight. Toss before serving.

Aunt Helen's West Indies Salad

This is a recipe I got from Bobby's Aunt Helen just after we got married. It is really simple and can be used as a salad served over fresh lettuce or stuffed in a ripe fresh tomato or as an appetizer served with crackers. It's very fresh and the crabmeat is not masked by a lot of other flavors.

1 medium onion chopped
2 Bay leaves
Salt and Pepper
6 ounces cider vinegar
3 ounces Wesson oil
4 ounces ice water
1/2 cup fresh chopped parsley
1 pound fresh picked lump or backfin crabmeat

Layer the crabmeat and onions in a dish sprinkling lightly with salt and pepper.

Put a couple of bay leaves in each layer as well as a sprinkling of the parsley.

Mix vinegar, oil and water and pour over crabmeat mixture.

Refrigerate overnight.

Southern women see no contradiction in mixing strength with gentleness.
—Sharon McKern

Sue's Shrimp Macaroni Salad

1 pound peeled boiled shrimp
1 8 ounce box of cooked and drained elbow macaroni
3/4 cup of sweet salad cubes
1/4 cup of diced celery
1 medium onion diced
2 hard boiled eggs diced
Salt and pepper
Mayonnaise

Mix all of the ingredients together with mayonnaise to your desired consistency. This is better if made a day ahead.

Sour Cream Fruit Salad

We used to have this all of the time and I miss it. I'm making it again.

1 cup fresh orange segments
1 cup crushed pineapple, drained
1 cup sweet shredded coconut
1 cup mini marshmallows
1 cup sour cream
1 jar maraschino cherries, drained
1/2 cup toasted pecans

Mix all ingredients together and chill.

Our Chicken Salad

I wasn't quite sure where to put this recipe. It can be an appetizer, a sandwich, a main dish so you will have to choose. I have made chicken salad this way for as long as I can remember. It's the way my grandmama and my mama make it and now the way that my daughters make it. We love it. And please, don't use salad dressing instead of mayonnaise!!

1 chicken boiled, remove skin and bones and chop into pieces
3 hard-cooked eggs, mashed up good (do not chop)
1/2 to 3/4 cup diced celery
3/4 to 1 cup of sweet pickle cubes
Hellman's Mayonnaise
Salt and Pepper
Fresh parsley if you have it on hand

Mix first four ingredients together.

Mix with mayonnaise to the desired consistency. (Be careful not to use too much mayo, you don't want it mushy)

When baking, follow directions. When cooking, go by your own taste.

—Laiko Bahr

Sweet & Sharp Pimento Cheese

Before I met Bobby I always bought my pimento cheese at the store, in the plastic container. Well that was short lived. His mama always made her pimento cheese from scratch and so for the last thirty some odd years, so have I. This is something, like the chicken salad, that is always on hand. If you go to a southern get together chances are you are going to have some pimento cheese.

My folks like it with pickle cubes and won't eat it any other way but you can leave them out if need be.

Note from Vicki

There are a few tips that you need to remember. Don't use a mild or rubbery cheddar. It's just not going to turn out right and don't use salad dressing, use mayonnaise.

Make sure the cheeses are at room temperature when you start to make this.

12 ounces sharp or extra sharp cheddar cheese grated
4 ounces (1/2 block) of cream cheese
1 jar diced pimentos
1 teaspoon sugar
3/4 cup of sweet salad cubes (drain off the liquid)
Mayonnaise

Mix the cheddar cheese and the cream cheese together with all of the other ingredients.

Add mayonnaise to the desired consistency. Add a little at a time.

Kristen's Melon Salad

My youngest daughter was bedridden after a back operation and this is about the only thing she wanted to eat. The first day home she wanted fruit salad, but the fruit and melon I got from the store weren't all that ripe so I made the mint syrup to pour over it since I had mint overtaking my herb garden. Now whenever I make fruit salad she thinks it isn't finished until the syrup is added. She ate this everyday for six weeks!

Cut up pieces of watermelon, cantaloupe and honeydew melon and mix with strawberries, grapes, and fresh pineapple cubes. Put in a large bowl and chill.

Mix 1 cup of water with 1 cup of sugar and bring to a boil. Remove from the heat and add ½ cup of fresh mint leaves. Put in the refrigerator until cool.

Pour the syrup mixture over the fruit and serve. (You will not need to use all of the syrup. The amount needed will depend on how much fruit you have.)

Old Fashioned Clam Chowder

This is the way folks around here have made clam chowder for years. No milk, no tomatoes. This is great with a pan of cornbread on a cold winter day.

About 1/4 pound fatback, diced
1 large onion, diced
4 medium red potatoes, diced
1 (8 ounce) bottle clam juice
Pepper
2 dozen shucked clams (chopped), with liquid

Fry out the fatback over medium-high heat, and cook until crisp. Remove pieces, and set aside.

Sauté the onions in the fatback grease until softened.

Add in the potatoes and black pepper.

Pour in the bottle of clam juice and the juice from the clams.

Simmer until potatoes are tender. About 15 minutes.

Add clams to the pot and cook for 5 minutes.

Serve with the crispy fatback pieces sprinkled over the top.

Sinfully Rich Sook Crab Soup

1 large onion minced fine
1 stick butter
1 cup flour
5 cups half & half
2 cups whipping cream
1 pound fresh backfin crabmeat free of shell
1/8 teaspoon freshly ground nutmeg
1/2 cup good sherry
Salt and pepper to taste

In a large saucepan melt the butter and cook the onion until translucent.

Add the flour and cook for 2 to 3 minutes.

Slowly pour in the half & half and the cream.

Add the crabmeat to the mixture and cook over very low heat for 30 minutes. Watch closely as this mixture can scorch easily.

Take off of heat and stir in the sherry, nutmeg and salt & pepper.

Character is what you are; reputation is what you try to make people think you are.

—Anonymous

Bairds Creek Crab Bisque

I love the seafood bisque at several of the coastal restaurants so I came up with this version.

2 tablespoons of very, very, finely minced onion
2 tablespoons of very, very, finely mined celery
1/2 cup butter
3 tablespoons flour
1 teaspoon salt
2 bay leaves
1/2 teaspoon paprika
1 quart whole milk
1/4 cup fresh chopped parsley
1 pound backfin crabmeat free of shell

Melt the butter in a large saucepan and sauté the onion and celery over low heat until very soft. Do not brown.

Blend in the flour, salt, paprika and add the bay leaves.

Add milk and cook until thickened.

Remove the bay leaves.

Stir in crabmeat and parsley.

Cook until crabmeat is heated through.

Carolina Corn Chowder

I got this recipe from a fellow I worked with for a while. He loved to cook and he would make this chowder and bring it in a crock pot to work. It was a big hit. It's a perfect dish for lunch on a cold winter day.

2 cups of sliced smoked sausage
1 medium diced onion
1 cup carrots diced
2 1 pound bags of frozen corn
4 cans chicken stock
1 pint half and half
1 small box wild rice (cook ahead)

Brown sausage in a heavy soup pot.

Add onion and carrots and cook for 5 minutes.

In food processor combine 1 can of chicken stock and 1/2 bag of corn. Process until smooth and add to sausage and vegetable mixture.

Add remaining corn and chicken stock and cook for 15 minutes. Then add the pint of half and half and already cooked wild rice.

Heat through and enjoy!

Vegetable Beef Soup

I love to make a big pot of this soup on a cold winter day. You may also add a handful of elbow macaroni or other vegetables that you might have on hand.

1/4 cup olive oil
1 1/2 pounds beef stew meat cut into small pieces
1 medium chopped onion
2 cloves garlic, chopped
1 small can of tomato paste
3 cans beef or chicken broth
1 teaspoon Worcestershire sauce
2 teaspoons salt
2 teaspoons black pepper
1 bay leaf
2 large cans diced tomatoes
1 cup sliced carrots,
2 stalks sliced celery
3 white potatoes diced into chunks
2 sweet potatoes diced into chunks
1 small bag frozen green beans
1 bag frozen corn
1 small bag of butter beans

In a large soup pot brown the meat in the olive oil. Add the onion and garlic and cook until the onion is translucent.

Add the tomato paste and stir into the meat and onion, cook for 1 to 2 minutes.

Note from Vicki

Take a large zip lock plastic bag and put your leftover vegetables in it. Keep this in the freezer and just keep adding to it when you have vegetables that are leftover. The next time you make soup, add the frozen ingredients.

Stewed Potato Soup

When I'm not feeling well my mother still makes this soup for me.

1 small diced onion
2 tablespoons butter
1/2 teaspoon salt
1/4 teaspoon pepper
2 cups of small diced potatoes
Water
1 tablespoon flour
1 tablespoon fresh chopped parsley

Sauté the onion in the butter until translucent.

Add the potatoes to the pot and cover with water.

Add the salt & pepper.

Cook until the potatoes are tender.

Mix the tablespoon of flour with enough water to make a paste and mix into the soup.

Stir in the parsley.

Cook about 5 more minutes.

"There is no love sincerer than the love of food."

—George Bernard Shaw

"Takin' In"

On the three mile long dirt road where I grew up there was a handful of small farmers, most of them related to one another, and they all grew a little tobacco. My Granddaddy Alton was one of those farmers, and when you arrived at the age when you could reach to the top of the tobacco cart you were expected to work. I didn't really mind working in tobacco. The part I didn't like, was having to get up so early during my summer off from school, but I was getting paid. I remember the first check I got. A check for seven dollars for a whole days work! I was thrilled! It was fun at the barn with all of the neighborhood women talking about whoever didn't happen to be there. I learned all kinds of things working those summers at the tobacco barn.

In the mornings those first few carts would be wet and full of dew. We would cut arm holes and a hole for our head in a trash bag and tie it around the waist with a piece of tobacco twine. Sometimes someone would sling it right in your face and you'd get an eyeful of tobacco juice, which can be a little irritating. About 11:00, things would dry off and you start getting sticky, gummy hands. I must admit though I liked the smell of the green tobacco. Every now and then there would be a big ole fat tobacco worm crawling on a leaf, and if we had one of those smart-alecky boys in the field, they would sometimes throw a dead snake in amongst the leaves to scare us.

Each of the farmers had a day to take in. Granddaddy's day was Tuesday, and all of the same people worked each farm. We would have to pack our dinner (in the south, its breakfast, dinner and supper) to take with us and Grandma Velma always brought mine. She would always have me a nice sandwich and a piece of cake fixed and of course the farm owner would always supply us with a drink (that's what we call any kind of soda or soft drink). We would get a drink mid-morning and then one at lunch if you didn't go home to eat. The farm owner would come around in the morning and ask you what kind of drink you wanted. I usually got a Mountain Dew or a Pepsi and some of the older ladies would get a short Co-Cola. I thought they were getting a raw deal but they said those short ones tasted better. And by the way, you just got one drink, no cooler full of ice with drinks to choose from, no ma'am. You order your drink, he goes to the store and brings it back for you, no extras.

On Tuesdays, when we worked at Granddaddy's, dinner was a little different. I guess Granddaddy liked to make sure his primers (which were my cousins or some of the other farmer's son's) were well fed so they would work hard to get the whole field primed. You couldn't get it "almost done" and come back the next day because you had to go to another farm. Anyway, I don't know how she did it but my Grandma always had a table full of food laid out every Tuesday. It started at 5:30 with breakfast for fellas that worked in the field priming the tobacco. It was a full fledged breakfast too, biscuits, grits, sausage and eggs with big pitchers of orange juice and fresh milk. After serving the field hands (and me and Grand-daddy too) she would get the dishes cleaned up and head out to the barn. At 7:00 a.m. we were at the barn, her looping the tobacco and me handing. Granddaddy always timed it so he and the boys would be back at the barn at noon. Me and Grandmama would walk up to the house with Granddaddy and the boys. Most of the women either went home or just sat at the barn and ate what they had packed for themselves. The boys would gather around the outdoor spigot with a bar of soap trying to get that tobacco gum off of their hands and splashin' their faces with the cold water.

Meanwhile back in the house I was helping Grandma set the food on the table which had already been set with plates, napkins, silverware and glasses. No paper plates or plastic cups for her, and the only dishwasher in sight was the two of us. When we first came in she had gotten a pan of fresh made biscuits out of the refrigerator and slipped them in the oven. The food she had cooked early that morning was all wrapped up on the stove in layers of kitchen towels, still warm as toast. We laid that table out with those fresh from the oven biscuits, crispy fried chicken, smoked picnic, potato salad, a big pot of speckled butter beans (which my sister always called 'backer beans) with boiled potatoes and okra, collards, a big bowl of stewed corn, fresh sliced tomatoes from the garden, cucumbers in vinegar, fresh sliced bell pepper from the garden, preserves and a cake, usually pineapple, because that was Granddaddy's favorite, AND let's not forget 2 big pitchers of cold sweet tea.

Thinking about it now, I just can't imagine how she did it, but she did, without one complaint and with a smile on her face. You can pretty well guess that my Granddaddy didn't have any problem getting primers for his field.

After lunch, and before we went back out to the barn to finish the day, all of the dishes would be washed and dried and the leftovers covered and put away.

Depending on the crop, we were usually done in the fields by about 3:00. When the last cartful was tied and stacked the women would say their goodbyes and head on home. Now it was time to hang the tobacco in the barn. I would pick up a stick full of the stacked tobacco and hand it to Grandmama, she would hand it to someone through the tobacco barn door, they would hoist it up to Grand-daddy who was usually on the first set of tier poles and he would hoist it up to one of the younger fellows who was hanging them at the top. This was rather monotonous work but there was always a lively conversation going on about one thing or another. Finally we would get done and me and Grandmama would head to the house, clean up and I'd help her get supper on the table. It was hard work but all the same, we were around the people we loved, smiling and laughing and having a good time and making memories we didn't know we were making.

The Main Course Seafood

Crabs, Shrimp, Oysters & Fish

Crab Pots, Oriental North Carolina

"So if anybody wants to get me something, get me 60 crabs—one for each year. I don't want no diamonds, I don't want no shoes, I don't want no party. I want some crabs!"

—Patti LaBelle on her 60th Birthday

"The Oyster"

Ah, the oyster, one of my favorite things. Ice cold, salty, and raw on the half shell is by far the best way to eat an oyster.

During the winter we regularly buy a bushel of oysters and eat off of them every afternoon when we get home from work. What a treat! How lucky we are to be able to have access to this wonderful thing, right at our back door. The Pamlico County area, where we live, is rich in all kinds of seafood and produces some wonderful oysters.

It was a normal thing almost every winter week-end to go to someone's house for an oyster roast. Get out the saw horses, top them with plywood and dump on the pots of steamed oysters. Some saltine crackers, butter, vinegar, hot sauce and catsup, and you can eat all night. Add some cold beer, and Pepsi for the kids and you've got one heck of a party. I've got some great oyster recipes in this book, but personally, I'm still a raw oyster girl.

"As I ate the oysters with their strong taste of the sea and their faint metallic taste that the cold white wine washed away, leaving only the sea taste and the succulent texture, and as I drank their cold liquid from each shell and washed it down with the crisp taste of the wine, I lost the empty feeling and began to be happy, and to make plans."

—Ernest Hemingway in "A Moveable Feast"

Carolina Fried Oysters

I like my oysters really crispy and I find that the rice flour gives you a crispier coating than just regular flour.

Fresh shucked oysters
2 beaten eggs
1 cup corn meal
1 cup rice flour
1 teaspoon salt
1/2 teaspoon black pepper
2 cups shortening for deep frying
1/4 cup bacon grease

Add the oysters to the beaten eggs. Mix the corn meal, rice flour, salt and pepper together. Remove the oysters from the egg mixture and cover them with the cornmeal mixture.

Melt the shortening with the bacon grease.

Shake off excess meal from oysters, drop into hot oil and fry until golden brown.

Drain on paper towels.

"A loaf of bread, the Walrus said,
Is what we chiefly need:
Pepper and vinegar besides
Are very good indeed—
Now if you're ready, Oysters, dear,
We can begin to feed!"

—Lewis Carroll (Charles Lutwidge Dodgson) (1832-1898)
Alice Through the Looking-Glass

What a Life!

Crabbin off the dock, swimmin' in the creek, eatin' mama's cookin'....

Scalloped Oysters

Don't overcook this. You want it to be moist not dry, almost like a pudding. This dish is always on my table for Christmas dinner.

2 (12-ounce) containers fresh oysters
2 eggs beaten
1 1/4 cups half-and-half
2 cups butter cracker crumbs
1 stick of butter, melted
1 teaspoon Worcestershire sauce
3/4 teaspoon salt
1 teaspoon hot sauce
1/4 teaspoon pepper
2 tablespoons chopped fresh parsley

Preheat oven to 350°.

Sprinkle ½ cup of the cracker crumbs in a greased 8-inch baking dish. Layer half each of oysters, salt, pepper, butter, and cracker crumbs in dish. Repeat layers.

Combine eggs, half-and-half, Worcestershire sauce, hot sauce, mix well. Pour over oyster mixture.

Sprinkle with parsley.

Bake for 35 minutes or until lightly browned.

Carolina Shrimp

The water's of North Carolina are abundant with this delicacy. According to *North Carolina Sea Grant and the North Carolina Fisheries Association,* in 2005 North Carolina Fishermen harvested 2.35 million pounds of shrimp, which at that time, was the third highest landing of shrimp on record.

We have three shrimp species in North Carolina.

- Brown Shrimp, whose shell is a reddish brown color, is a muddy bottom shrimp, but can also be found in sandy bottoms and is more active at night. The Brown Shrimp season is usually late summer and fall. This shrimp is North Carolina's most abundant shrimp.

- Pink Shrimp, or what we call Spotted Shrimp, burrow into the bottom during the day, and like the Brown Shrimp, will be more active at night. These shrimp are usually caught during April, May and June.

- White Shrimp, or what we call Green-Tails, like soft muddy bottoms and brackish water. They usually show up around August and will drop off around November.

So which one is the best? You will have to judge for yourself. I love them all and always make sure that my freezer gets packed to the rim every year.

Shrimp are graded by count, so when you buy them, the smaller the number, the bigger the shrimp. For instance, I usually try to buy a 21/25 count which means there are 21 to 25 shrimp in a pound. Overall, I think this is the perfect eating size.

So how do you pick a good shrimp? It should have relatively no smell, it should feel firm, not mushy or soft.

Fried Shrimp

Good old fried shrimp. We eat shrimp at least once a week at my house. It's plentiful, it's delicious and can be cooked a hundred different ways, but sometimes the simplest is just what you're looking for. Fried shrimp is definitely Bobby's favorite way to eat shrimp. He always has me cook just a few more than we might eat so he can eat them the next morning for breakfast.

As many shrimp as you think you can eat, (plus a few more) shelled and deveined
2 cups plain corn meal
2 teaspoons salt
1 teaspoon pepper
Vegetable or peanut oil for frying

Heat about one inch of oil in a frying pan. Bring up to medium high heat. Mix the cornmeal, salt and pepper together in a large zip lock bag. Put the shrimp in the bag and shake. Make sure all of the shrimp have a good light coating. Fry the shrimp in the hot oil until pink. Don't overcook.

Oh Baby Shrimp Scampi

Why do I call this "Oh Baby Shrimp Scampi"? Because every time I make it Bobby just eats and eats and keeps saying "Oh Baby"!

1 tablespoon Kosher Salt
1 pound linguine or spaghetti

In a large pot of boiling water, add the salt and linguini. Cook according to directions.

1 stick of butter
2 tablespoons olive oil
3 cloves minced garlic
1 small shallot (or onion if you don't have it)
1/2 cup of white wine
      (whatever you're drinking or have on hand)
1 pound shrimp peeled and deveined
      (I use 21-25's, we like good size shrimp)
1 teaspoon Old Bay
1 tablespoon hot sauce (Texas Pete)
1/2 teaspoon freshly ground black pepper
1/2 cup chopped fresh parsley
Juice from 2 lemons

Melt the butter and olive oil over medium-low heat. Add the shallot. Sauté until soft then add the garlic and sauté for 1 minute. Add the white wine and simmer for 5 minutes. Add the shrimp, Old Bay, salt, and pepper and sauté until the shrimp have just turned pink, about 5 minutes. Remove from heat, add the parsley, lemon juice, and hot sauce. Toss to combine. Add the cooked pasta to the sauce and toss well.

Everyday Shrimp

Most people would say this is just plain boiled shrimp—but I don't bring my shrimp to a boil. I bring the liquid and spices I'm going to cook the shrimp in to a boil and when I add the shrimp I turn the fire down to low. Just a slow simmer until they turn pink. That's the perfect everyday shrimp.

2 pounds of shrimp (cleaned or in the shell, your preference)
5 cups of water
1 lemon, cut in slices
2 bay leaves
1 tablespoon salt
1 tablespoon Old Bay
1 tablespoon vinegar

Bring the water, lemon, bay leaves, Old Bay, salt and vinegar to a boil. Boil for 3 minutes.

Ass all of the shrimp and turn the fire to low.

When shrimp turn a dark pink remove them from the liquid.

May be served hot or cold.

Serve with Red Sauce or White Champagne Sauce.

Shrimp and Crab

This is really rich and really good. It's nice to serve for company. You can also use this as an appetizer, just put in a chafing dish and serve with crackers. (You might want to cut the shrimp into pieces if you are going to serve as an appetizer.)

1 stick butter
1/2 cup flour
1/2 cup milk
1/2 cup white wine
1/2 cup grated parmesan cheese
Juice from one lemon
Salt & pepper to taste
2 teaspoons hot sauce
1 pound cooked shrimp
1 pound backfin crabmeat (picked thru for shell)
1/2 sleeve of Ritz™ crackers crushed
2 tablespoons butter

Melt the butter in a heavy bottom saucepan. Add flour and cook for about 2 minutes. Stir in milk, wine, cheese, lemon juice, salt and pepper and hot sauce. Cook until thick. Remove from heat.

Gently stir in the shrimp and the crabmeat.

Preheat oven to 350°.

Grease a 9 x 13 glass baking dish and put in the seafood mixture.

Layer the cracker crumbs on top and dot with butter.

Bake for 15 minutes.

Pamlico Paella

This is a really impressive dish and you've got everything right there in one pan. Make a small salad and some French bread and your meal is done. Don't be afraid to improvise with whatever seafood you might have on hand. Try adding mussels, lobster or even firm fish. Don't be afraid to give this a try for your next get together.

6 to 8 blue crabs, cleaned, backs & apron removed and split in half.

Steam Crabs in 1 inch of water with 1 Tablespoon of Old Bay until <u>almost</u> done. Set Aside.

3 cups chicken stock (more if needed)
1 chicken, cut in small pieces
Salt and pepper
1/4 cup olive oil
4 garlic cloves, crushed
1 red bell pepper cut in 1 inch strips
1 can of artichoke hearts (Not marinated or pickled)
1 onion, diced
1 bay leaf
2 ripe tomatoes, peeled, seeded and finely chopped
1 1/2 cups medium grain white rice (Do not use long grain rice)
1 teaspoon saffron threads
1 1/2 pounds of large shrimp peeled and deveined
1 pound sea scallops
1 dozen clams, cleaned (in the shell)
1/2 cup sweet peas, fresh or frozen (don't use canned)
1 lemon

In a saucepan bring the chicken stock to a boil. Lower to simmer and add saffron. Make sure the stock is well seasoned.

Season the chicken with salt and pepper. Heat the olive oil in a paella pan or wide skillet. Brown the chicken on all sides until almost done. Remove the chicken from the pan.

Drain out excess oil and sauté the garlic, onion, red pepper and artichoke hearts until tender. Remove from pan.

Add the tomato to the pan and sauté until the water has cooked out and the mixture has turned thick (about 10 minutes). Add the rice, stirring to coat the grains. Pour in the simmering stock. As the stock comes to a boil layer the vegetables, chicken, clams and crabs around the pan submerging below the liquid as much as possible. DO NOT STIR from this point on.

Cook on medium high for about 10 minutes then reduce the heat to medium low. Simmer until all of the liquid has been absorbed (about 10 more minutes). Check to see if the rice is done. If not add more broth and cook a few minutes more. Arrange the shrimp and scallops around the pan. Sprinkle peas over the top. Cover with foil. Cook for another 2 to 3 minutes.

(The rice should start to caramelize on the bottom which is what you want. This is called the socarrat. Be careful not to burn).

Remove from heat and keep covered for at least another 5 minutes. Remove foil. Squeeze lemon over the top. Dig in.

Pride of the Neuse Shrimp and Grits

For Grits:
2 cups water
1 1/2 cups milk
1 teaspoon salt
1 cup quick cooking grits (Not Instant)
1 stick butter.
In a saucepan, bring water, milk, and salt to a boil. Slowly stir in grits until well mixed. Return to a boil, cover pot with a lid, lower to simmer, and cook for approximately 30 minutes stirring frequently. Add more water if necessary. Stir in butter.

For Shrimp:
1 pound Neuse River shrimp, peeled and deveined (21-25 count)
6 slices bacon, chopped
1/4 cup chopped onion
1 clove garlic, minced
Juice from 2 lemons
3 tablespoons chopped parsley
1 tomato diced

Fry chopped bacon in pan until crispy. Remove bacon from pan. Add onion and garlic until soft. Add shrimp and cook until pink. Remove from the heat.

Add the lemon juice, parsley and chopped tomato. Mix well and serve over grits

> "Do not overcook this dish. Most seafoods … should be simply threatened with heat and then celebrated with joy."

> —Jeff Smith (The Frugal Gourmet)—I agree wholeheartedly with
> Jeff! *Vicki*

China Grove Stuffed Shrimp

This is another one of those recipes where I got in a hurry and didn't have time to make what I had planned and didn't have the right ingredients to make my second choice. So I came up with this in about 5 minutes and I think its one of the best dishes I ever made. The oranges give it a fantastic flavor. Everyone loves it.

<u>Stuffing:</u>
1 pound backfin crabmeat free of shell
1 egg
1 teaspoon Worcestershire
1 teaspoon hot sauce
1/2 teaspoon Old Bay seasoning
1/2 cup mayonnaise
1/2 cup fresh chopped parsley
1/2 sleeve buttery crackers, crushed

2 pounds large shrimp cleaned and butterflied, (leave tails on)
3 or 4 large oranges, sliced into 1/2 inch slices
1/2 cup melted butter

Preheat oven to 400°.

Mix the ingredients for the stuffing together until well blended. Butterfly the shrimp and stuff each one with about 1 to 2 tablespoons of the stuffing mixture.

Lay the stuffed shrimp on a baking sheet lined with the oranges and drizzle with the butter.

Bake for about 7 to 10 minutes, turn shrimp, drizzle the other side with butter and return until shrimp are done. About another 3 to 5 minutes.

Put on a serving platter with lemons and oranges for garnish.

Stuffed Flounder Filets

This is a very simple dish. It goes back to my thinking that the less you do with it, the better it is.

Clean your fish and filet them. Cut down the center of each filet so that you will have 4 pieces per fish.

Backfin crabmeat, free of shell
Salt and pepper
Melted butter
Lemon

The amounts in this recipe depend on how many filets you have.

Preheat oven to 375°.

Take one flounder filet and lay it out flat, sprinkle with salt and pepper.

Put a layer of crabmeat on top of the filet and drizzle liberally with melted butter.

Roll up the filet and secure with a toothpick.

Repeat until all filets are stuffed.

Place the fish in a baking pan and drizzle generously with butter and lemon juice.

Bake for 20 minutes or until filets are flaky.

Fried Ocracoke Blue Fish

Blue fish that have been caught that day, cleaned and filleted
Salt and Pepper
Fine ground corn meal
Peanut Oil

Clean the fish.

(Don't refrigerate unless you absolutely have to).

Sprinkle each side lightly with salt & pepper. Dredge in corn meal. Fry in hot oil until golden.

Our whole family LOVES going to Ocracoke! Where else can you find miles of beach with no houses, no condos, no nothing! It's like we stepped back in time. Thank goodness someone saw fit to protect the beautiful natural seashore so generations to come can enjoy its beauty. If you want to relax, take your 4-wheel drive down to the beach and just look and listen to the surf. It relaxes me just thinking about it.

There is nothing better than going out surf fishing, or out in the boat and catching a mess of blue fish.

The secret to good blue fish though is to cook them immediately. Don't wait a day. Just go home, clean the fish and get the oil hot.

I also don't like to mask the flavor of the fish with breader mixes. I think it takes away from the natural flavor of the fish.

Whatever you had planned for supper that day can wait until tomorrow. FRESH FISH, now this is really good eating.

Daddy's Fish Stew

This recipe is very simple to make with not a lot of ingredients and it is fantastic. And don't turn your nose up at the eggs. People will fight over them they're so good. Now Daddy used to put so much black pepper in it you would have thought he owned stock in the pepper company, so I toned mine down a little. You make yours as hot as you like.

4 to 5 slices fat back, diced
1 large rock fish or other firm fish, cut into 1 to 2 inch chunks
2 onions, cut into rounds and separated
8 to 10 potatoes cut into 1 inch chunks
Salt & Pepper
1 large can of Campbell's Tomato Soup
Water
Eggs

In a large stock pot cook the fatback slices until crisp.

Start layering onions, potatoes and fish in that order sprinkling lightly with salt & pepper between each layer. After all layers are made, mix the tomato soup with enough water to cover the layers and gently pour into pot.

Simmer approximately 30 minutes or until potatoes are done.

Break eggs one at a time into the simmering pot. Cover and cook another 5 to 10 minutes.

Serve with cornbread and you have one fantastic meal.

Zack Bruno showing off his catch of the day.

"Carolina Blue Crabs"

It doesn't get much better that a big pile of just steamed Carolina Blue Crabs. The meat it so sweet and succulent it's just hard to resist.

The male hard crabs are called Jimmies and the females are called Sooks. Some people will tell you that if you're going to steam crabs you should just buy Jimmie crabs. I have to say, I don't agree. Now Jimmie crabs are usually bigger but I've had some big fat female crabs that are just as good.

Crabs do have somewhat of a grading system. For instance if you ask for Number One Jimmies, you will get the biggest and best. Number Two Jimmies will be a smaller less meaty crab and if you get Number Threes you get a mix of Jimmies and Sooks (mostly Sooks) but still good eating.

Male Crab—Jimmie

Female Crab—Sook

Fried Hard Crabs

You don't see a lot of people frying hard crabs anymore, but my grandma used to do it a lot. If you don't mind eatin' through the shell it's a good old fashioned meal.

Get as many blue crabs as you think you're going to eat and then double it. Clean the crabs, removing the legs, shell, dead man fingers and apron. Cut the crabs in half. Put on a cutting board and flatten out with a mallet, frying pan or a covered brick. (hit 'em hard!)

Sprinkle the crabs with salt and pepper and dredge in flour. Fry in hot oil until golden brown. About 7 to 10 minutes on medium high.

Crabmeat and Rice

1 pound fresh backfin crabmeat
1 stick butter
1/2 teaspoon Old Bay seasoning
1/2 teaspoon hot sauce
1 1/2 cups sour cream
1/2 cup chopped fresh parsley
Salt & pepper

3 or 4 cups of cooked white rice

Sauté the crabmeat in the butter and then add the other ingredients. Heat through and serve over rice.

Steamed Jimmies

Get a large steamer pot. Put about two inches of water in the bottom along with a cut up lemon, 6 bay leaves and ¼ cup Old Bay seasoning. Put your LIVE crabs in the steamer basket and steam for about 20 minutes. Crabs should be a nice orange color.

How do you eat them?

Get a big pitcher of iced tea, or cold beer, a roll of paper towels and a knife (optional). Get a bucket for the shells.

Reach in the bowl and get you a big fat crab. The heavier the crab is the more meat you're going to get. Pull off the big claws and set aside. DON'T throw these away, we're going to get back to them.

Turn the crab over and tear off the apron. Turn it over again and tear off the shell. These come off really easily. Throw them in the shell bucket. Pull out the dead mans fingers (its just the lungs) and throw them in the shell bucket. That yellow stuff that you might think looks gross is the fat, and a lot of people will tell you to throw it out, but don't, it's good. Eat it.

Break the body in half. Break off the top leg and twist, you should get a big chunk of meat.

Take a knife (or some people just use their fingers) and split each half of the crab horizontally, this will expose chambers of crabmeat. Pick out the meat.

Suck out the little piece of meat at the end of each leg when you tear it off.

Now go back to the claw. Just below what I call the pincher, take a knife and score it on one side. Take the claw in both hands and break where you made the score. If you did it right, all of the meat from that end of the claw will come out attached to the pincher end. There is also a little meat in the other end of the claws, so cut it open. Don't let anything go to waste. It's way too good.

Keep repeating the process until you're full. This might take a while.

My husband, Bobby, gives lessons on how to eat steamed crabs. There is a technique, but I say, dig in and get at it any way you can because it's definitely worth it.

Fried Soft Shell Crabs

What a delicacy. Nothing much better than a fat, fried soft shell crab. You can dress him up or dress him down. Serve him as a main course with a little dill sauce on the side or slap him between a hamburger bun with some lettuce, tomato and tartar sauce. Either way, he'll be delicious.

6 to 8 cleaned soft shell crabs
2 beaten eggs
1/2 cup milk
1 cup cornmeal
1/4 cup corn starch
1 1/2 teaspoons salt
1 teaspoon black pepper
Peanut Oil for frying

Lay the crabs on a paper towels and gently press with more paper towels to remove as much water as possible.

Beat the two eggs with the milk in a bowl. Blend the cornmeal and cornstarch with the salt and pepper in another bowl.

Drench the crabs in the egg mixture and then dredge in the cornmeal mixture.

Drop into hot oil and fry on each side about 2 minutes or until golden brown.

Note from Vicki

When you put the crabs in the hot oil ... Stand Back! If they have any water in them they are going to pop and that hot oil burns! I know this from experience (I can show you the scars).

Soft Shell Crabs

I think this is my favorite way to eat soft shell crabs. Slathered in seasoned butter and grilled to perfection. These will really melt in your mouth.

Cleaned soft shell crabs
2 sticks butter
1 clove garlic
1 teaspoon Old Bay Seasoning™
1 bay leaf

In a small saucepan melt the butter and mix in the garlic, seasoning and bay leaf. Simmer over a very low heat for three minutes being careful not to brown the butter.

Over a medium grill, lay out your crabs and baste continually with the butter sauce. Cook on each side for about 3 to 5 minutes depending on how hot your grill is and how big your crabs are.

Note from Vicki

When picking out soft shell crabs, "reach out and touch". It's hard to tell just by looking if you've got a real soft shell or if you just have a paper shell. The best soft shell crabs will feel very soft and full and the "shell" will feel completely smooth.

Coastal Crab Stew

A big stew pot
12 Carolina Blue Crabs cleaned and split in half
3/4 cup of chopped fatback (salt pork) cut into small cubes
1/2 cup flour
1 cup chopped onion
5 or 6 white potatoes cut into 1 inch chunks
1 can of Snow's Clam Chowder™
Water
1/3 cup chopped parsley
1 (or more) tablespoons hot sauce
3 bay leaves
Salt and pepper
1 can of canned biscuits cut into fourths

Fry out the salt pork until crispy and remove from the fat.

Add ½ cup of flour to the fat and cook for 3 to 4 minutes over a medium low heat. Add 2 cups of water. Add the onions and cook until tender. Be careful not to burn the roux.

Turn the fire up to medium high and add the potatoes, chowder, parsley, hot sauce, bay leaves, salt & pepper, and enough water to make a creamy gravy (not too thick).

Cook for 10 minutes at a simmer.

Add the crabs to the pot, making sure they are covered by the gravy (add water if needed). Cook another 10 minutes, covered, over medium simmer. Add quartered biscuits making sure they get into the gravy. Cover and simmer for 5 to 10 more minutes.

Roll up your sleeves and dig in.

Down Home Boil

I use a big stainless steel pot that has a strainer insert in it to make this boil. A great dish for a crowd in the spring or summer. Pour it out on paper lined picnic tables and dig in. It's not only a great meal, its fun too.

4 bay leaves
2 heads of garlic cut in half
1/2 cup Old Bay seasoning
2 lemons sliced
4 chicken legs
4 chicken thighs
2 large chicken breasts cut in half
1 pound smoked sausage
3 onions cut in quarters
2 pounds of potatoes cut in quarters
6 sweet potatoes, washed well and cut into 1 inch slices
2 or 3 artichokes (depends on how many people like artichokes)
5 ears of corn cut in half
2 pounds of shrimp
1 dozen live blue crabs

In your large pot put 3 gallons of water, add the lemons, garlic, bay leaves and crab boil. NOTE: You may need to add more water throughout the process.

Bring this mixture to a simmer and add the chicken. Simmer the chicken for 10 minutes.

Add the sausage, onions, potatoes, sweet potatoes, artichokes and corn. Simmer covered for 10 to 15 minutes.

Put in the crabs and continue to cook for 15 minutes. Add shrimp and cook for another 5 minutes. Turn off heat, keep covered and let stand for 30 minutes before eating.

Pecan Scallops

You can use this recipe as a main dish or as an appetizer.

1/2 cup pecan halves
1/2 cup fresh chopped parsley
1 clove garlic
Zest of 1 lemon
Juice of 1 lemon
Salt and pepper
1 1/2 pounds sea scallops
Flour to dredge
1 tablespoon olive oil

In food processor, combine pecans, parsley, garlic, zest of lemon. Set aside.

Rinse and pat-dry scallops. Lightly season with salt and pepper. Roll scallops lightly in flour

Heat olive oil in large skillet over high heat.

Add scallops and sauté quickly, tossing frequently until golden and nearly cooked through—about 3 to 4 minutes.

Reduce heat to low. Add pecan mixture and cook 2 minutes.

Remove to serving plate and sprinkle with lemon juice.

Buttery Grilled Scallops

It is best to use large sea scallops for this recipe. Keep in mind the "less is more" theory here. If you cook the scallop too longs its will get tough and spongy, but if you do it right it will be soft, juicy and perfect.

1 to 2 pounds of large sea scallops
Skewers
2 sticks butter
1 clove garlic
Juice from one lemon
1/2 teaspoon salt
1/2 teaspoon ground black pepper
1 teaspoon Old Bay Seasoning™
1 bay leaf
1/4 cup chopped fresh parsley

Gently put the scallops on the skewers (if you are using wooden skewers soak them in water first).

In a small saucepan mix all of the remaining ingredients and over a very low heat cook for 3 minutes being careful not to brown the butter.

Place the scallops on a medium hot grill and baste liberally with the butter sauce. The grill needs to be hot to seal in the juices and to get some caramelization on the scallops.

Cook on each side for 2 to 3 minutes. Remove from skewers and serve with extra butter sauce.

Seafood Casserole

1 1/2 sticks of butter
1/2 cup diced celery
3/4 cup diced onion
1/2 cup chopped green pepper
1 cup fresh mushrooms sliced
1 to 1 1/2 cups of good mayonnaise
1 teaspoon Old Bay Seasoning™
2 tablespoons Worshtershire sauce
1 tablespoon hot sauce
2 eggs
2 cups fresh bread crumbs
Juice from two lemons
1 pound backfin or lump crabmeat (Do Not use claw meat)
1 1/2 pounds shrimp (cooked until halfway done)

Preheat oven to 350°.

Sauté onion, celery, pepper and mushrooms in the butter until soft.

Mix the sautéed vegetables with mayo, old bay, salt and pepper, hot sauce, eggs, breadcrumbs and lemon juice.

Fold in the crabmeat and shrimp.

Bake for 30 minutes.

"Newlywed Shrimping Trip"

It's a tradition around here. When shrimping season gets close you can see everybody getting their trawls out. Making sure there are no big holes torn in the net. Making sure the chain on the trawl doors is at the perfect length so they will open up perfectly. Getting the cull tray on the back of the boat and plenty of big baskets to hold the anticipated "haul". Oh it's a big time, and I don't just mean for those big trawlers. Every man who has at least a 16' boat with a motor on it is going out on opening day.

Let's go back about 30 years. Young, newly married and eager to spend time with my husband, Bobby, I enthusiastically agreed to go shrimping with him on opening day. Now it's not like I had never been before. I had gone out shrimping with my Daddy plenty of times. He would have me stand at the cull tray and pick out all of the little fish and throw them back over, put the shrimp in a basket and if there were any fat crabs I would have to put them in a five gallon bucket. I would wear a pair of his gloves which were about 6 sizes too big for me, and which did nothing to prevent the crabs from grabbing hold. I learned real quick just how to pick them up at the back so they couldn't get to my tender fingers. So anyway, I'm thinking, this will be fun, we can spend the day out on the water, I'll catch some rays and we'll have fresh shrimp for supper. The day finally arrives. My dear husband wakes me at 4:30AM (I should tell you that I am not a morning person, especially not a 4:30AM morning person). I get up and grab my new picnic basket I got for my shower and packed it with sandwiches, cheese, crackers, and fruit. I fixed a thermos of coffee and put two cute mugs inside and closed the lid. Oh this was going to be such a nice day.

It's late April, the first chance to catch the first spotted shrimp of the year, and the weather had been awfully nice all month. I wasn't quite sure but I thought I heard some thunder in the distance. I went to the door, it's dark as can be and when I opened it, cold air, and I mean really cold air, hit me in the face along with a wet, rainy, drizzle. Okay, so it's cold and rainy, this will still be fun. I go and put on another sweatshirt and pull on a pair of long underwear under my jeans. No good. Bobby comes in, takes one look at me, shakes his head and tells me I have to wear foul weather gear because of the rain and wind. Well, I don't have foul weather gear, so he goes out to the barn and comes back with what probably used to be a yellow slicker and a pair of bib overalls. Dirty, crabby smelling, and as stiff and hard as they were, I managed to get them on and we were on our way to the boat dock.

We get all of our gear on the boat. Gloves, food, chairs, two coolers, one filled with ice, four baskets and several five gallon buckets. The rain has ceased, but it's still cold and windy. I put my beach chair in, unfold it, wrap up in a blanket and settle back for the ride as we head out across the Neuse River to Adam's Creek. Along the way, I realize that everybody, and his brother too, are all headed for the same spot. Big boats, little boats, they were everywhere. The word was out that the shrimp were plentiful and everybody wanted their fair share.

As we headed into the creek Bobby called me to take the wheel. Okay no problem. I had driven a boat plenty of times. He heads to the back, getting everything just right and at first light he throws over the net, and tells me to give her some gas. I feel the pull on the boat as the doors spread out and the net comes tight. Our first tow and everything is going perfectly! No tangled up net, the doors opened just right and the sun had decided to shine.

After about ten minutes Bobby pulls in the try-net to see how we're doing and low and behold, that little net was almost full of shrimp. Well he gets all excited and tells me to "hold her straight". I slow the boat down and follow my orders, I certainly don't want to get that net tangled up. A few hundred yards ahead and to the right of me I see a big shrimp trawler, about 80 feet long, his outriggers down, he's just put his net out. I figure it might be a good idea to venture over to the left a little, but as I start to edge over I realize that there is another trawler, this one about 50 feet long, just off of my port stern. To my starboard there are two smaller boats about fifty yards behind me, so I can't pull in front of them, as they might run over our net. Bobby is busy pulling on a net packed full of shrimp and is thrilled with the catch. When he felt my *slight turn* of the boat he says, "You're doing a great job, baby, just keep her straight."

I look ahead and see that I am pinned in on all sides and the eighty foot big boy is almost dead ahead of me about fifty yards. "Honey," I say to Bobby, "there is this boat ahead of me and I'm going to have to stop." He never turns around, but says, unconcerned, "He'll move, you go just like you're going." I see the trawler on my port side is pulling in his nets and has slowed down so I'm now clear on that side. "Honey," I say again, somewhat excited, "I'm gonna' have to turn or I'm gonna' hit this boat!" I can see the captain in the pilot house glance my way as he gets ready to cross directly ahead of me. Again, Bobby never turns around but says, in an agitated voice, "He'll move Vicki, just stay straight!" I am almost frantic when I see the captain step out of the pilot house, look straight at me and throw his hands up in the air. I let go of the wheel and run to the back and take a seat in the safety of my beach chair. Bobby looks at me and says, "What are you doing, get back up there." I just looked at him, pointed and shook my head, *no way.* He finally decides to turn around and as he does he starts cussing and running at the same time. He grabs the wheel turns hard to port, and shoves the motor in reverse. The trawler misses hitting us by about ten feet. After several very stressful minutes he managed to get us out of the midst of that chaotic mass of boats. He finally settled down in his captain's chair, exhausted, and turns to look at me. "What in the hell were you thinking? That's an eighty foot trawler?" I just looked right back at him, "I told you he wouldn't move, you told me to stay straight and I did." Nothing more was said after that, but needless to say, I didn't drive the boat anymore that day and it was the very first and the very last shrimping trip I went on with my husband. He's never asked and I've never volunteered. So my advice for a happy marriage is "Don't go shrimping on opening day with the one you love."

The Main Course Beef, Chicken, Pork & Pasta

(and a few other things tossed in)

The harbor at Oriental, North Carolina

"I drive way too fast to worry about cholesterol."

—Steven Wright

Bobby Prescott fishing on Portsmouth Island

When you live on the coast, fishing is a favorite pastime, plus you get to recap the benefits of a great meal when you get home.

"Sundays in the South"

Sunday at our house meant two things. You were going to go to Sunday School and Church, and you were going to go eat dinner at your Grandmama's. In my case, it meant dinner at Grandma Velma's, and supper at Grandma Lotha's.

The church that we went to was about a mile down the road. You always dressed up. Paten leather shoes, lacy socks, frilly dresses, your hair curled and your body scrubbed clean from the dirt of playing outside all day on Saturdays. The absolute best that you had. My mama would make sure that my paten leather shoes were shiny by making me shine them with Vaseline the night before.

So off we would go to the church at the end of the road. In hand our little hand-kerchiefs with our "offering" of change tied up in it. We had friends at church and Sunday School was fun, but when the church service started you had better be quiet. No talking and no squirming in the seats. It just wasn't tolerated. After all, this was a no-nonsense, feet washing Original Free Will Baptist Church.

Of course you know it's hard for children to pay attention sometimes. So I took in everything that was around me. There were seven lights hanging from the ceiling of the church. They were shaped like columns and were a creamy color with some brown thrown in. Probably some kind of plastic or resin I would guess. I could tell you the names of every person on the newly dedicated stained glass windows and on what page you could find "There's power, power, wonder working power in the blood, of the lamb …" in the hymnal.

I loved putting my own dimes and nickels in the plate when it came around and seeing all of the pretty dresses that the ladies were wearing. I would keep an eye on all of the oldest men in the congregation to see who was going to nod off first. I loved it when I got to set behind Mrs. Kitty who was a beautiful lady that had one of those fox stoles. It was always positioned in a way that the fox with those glass eyes was looking right at me. It kept me mesmerized. And I dreamed about the day I could have one of those foxes around my neck but of course by the time I "came of age" they were long out of style.

After church we would usually go to my Grandmama Velma's house to eat dinner (my mama's mama). A full fledged Sunday dinner would usually consist of fried chicken, fresh collards or cabbage, potato salad, string beans or speckled butter beans, baked sweet potatoes, fresh stewed corn, cut up tomatoes, cucumbers and homemade biscuits. Of course there was always a cake for dessert with cow's cream on the side and Sweet Tea. After we would eat the adults would sit around talking about this and that until about 3 o'clock (we were playing or napping) and then we were off to my Grandma Lotha's or Mammy's house (they lived right down the road from each other) which was my Daddy's mama and grandmama.

At Grandma Lotha's there was always a pot of coffee brewing and whatever she had cooked for the day was covered on the stove. We just got a plate and helped ourselves.

She always had a big pan of those flat cathead clabber biscuits. She usually had a big pot of collards made and either a ham or some chicken and pastry and a big pitcher of sweet tea to wash it all down.

She had one of those melamine dining sets with the chrome and plastic covered seats. Everybody always just sat around that table and talked. I probably learned most of life's lessons from listening to the conversations at that table. They might get a little heated sometimes but Grandmama would just bring out her freshly made coconut cake and all would be well again.

We might walk down the dirt road to Mammy and Papa's house (my great-grandparents) and of course there was more food there. She, like her daughter, would have everything covered on the stove and whoever might be coming in or out would grab whatever they wanted.

Food was the way to show love. There was no money to buy presents or go places. You visited. You ate. You talked.

Your belly and your heart were both filled to the brim.

Vicki's Sweet Tea Fried Chicken

It's not Sunday in the South without fried chicken, or at least it didn't use to be. I probably fried a chicken every Sunday for the first 10 years I was married. There is just something that's comforting about fried chicken. Maybe it's because we grew up on it. "Hand the children a chicken leg and send them outside to play."

1 Large Cast Iron Frying Pan
1 fryer cut up into serving pieces
1 pitcher of sweet tea
2 eggs
1 cup buttermilk
1 tablespoon Texas Pete
2 cups AP flour
2 teaspoons salt
1 teaspoon pepper
1 or 2 cups Crisco shortening
2 tablespoons bacon grease

The night before you are going to cook the chicken, or at least early that morning, cut up your chicken, put in a large bowl and cover with the sweet tea, and set in the refrigerator.

Remove chicken pieces from the tea and in another large bowl mix the two eggs with the buttermilk and the Texas Pete. Add the chicken pieces and let them marinate at least an hour in the refrigerator.

Remove from the refrigerator and bring the chicken to room temperature. In a large zip top bag mix the flour, salt and pepper. Add the chicken a few pieces at a time and coat well.

In a large cast iron frying pan bring the Crisco and the bacon grease to a medium heat. Add the chicken pieces (don't crowd the pan). COVER. Fry until golden brown on one side. Turn chicken pieces over and fry UNCOVERED until golden and juices run clear.

Chicken and Pastry

There seems to be a misunderstanding among some people regarding chicken and dumplings and chicken and pastry. Well here's my take. Pastry is thin and dumplings are plump.

1 chicken	1 teaspoon salt
Water	1 teaspoon black pepper
1 celery rib, sliced	1 bay leaf
1 medium onion, diced	1 teaspoon thyme
1 cup sliced baby carrots	

1 can of Campbell's cream of chicken soup

Pastry:

2 cups all-purpose flour	1 teaspoon salt
2 tablespoons shortening or lard	1/4 cup cold water

In a heavy pot with a lid place the chicken, celery, onion, carrots, salt, pepper, bay leaf and poultry seasoning. Cover with water. Simmer all over low heat until tender, about 1 hour. Let chicken cool slightly in pot, then remove and take the meat off of the bones. Return the chicken meat to the pot. Add the cream of chicken soup and simmer over low heat while making the dumplings.

In a medium bowl, cut the shortening into the flour and salt. Stir in 1/4 cup water (add more if needed) to form a soft dough. Roll out dough on a floured surface, until about 1/8 of an inch thick (you can do this ahead, put between waxed paper and freeze). Cut into 1 inch wide strips using a pizza cutter or knife. Tear off pieces and drop into simmering broth. Simmer for 15 to 20 minutes. The last 10 minutes cover the pot.

Note from Vicki

If you are short on time, go buy a package of Anne's Frozen Pastry™. It really is just as good as homemade.

Fettuccine Chicken Alfredo

1 cup broccoli cut into pieces
2 tablespoons butter
1 pound skinless boneless chicken breast cut into strips
1 can cream of mushroom soup
1/2 cup milk
1/2 cup Parmesan cheese
Salt and pepper

Prepare fettuccine according to package directions.

Add broccoli to the pasta water for the last 5 minutes of cooking time. Drain.

In large skillet heat butter and cook chicken until browned.

Add soup, milk, cheese, pepper.

Stir in fettuccine and broccoli.

Serve immediately.

Chicken, Rice and Dumplings

This was an absolute staple when I was growing up. We ate chicken and rice a lot. If you made chicken salad you didn't dare discard that stock afterward, you put in a couple of cups of rice and there's a whole other meal. I still do that today when I make chicken salad. I just can't let that great stock go to waste.

1 chicken cut into pieces
Water to cover
Salt and Pepper
2 cans chicken stock
1 medium onion chopped
1 stalk celery chopped
1 cup sliced carrots
1 cup rice (uncooked)
1 container canned biscuits

Wash chicken and place in stockpot. Cover with water, season with salt and pepper, and simmer for 30 minutes.

Add onion, celery and carrots. Cook another 20 minutes or until chicken is tender.

You can then leave chicken on the bone or remove and take chicken off of the bone and add back to the pot.

Add chicken stock and rice. When rice is done flatten out the biscuits and drop into simmering pot (you may need to add more liquid).

Dumplings will plump up in liquid. Cook for about 10 more minutes and you will have the perfect comfort food.

Roasted Duck with Cherry Sauce

A friend of mine cooked this duck for us one Christmas. We had never had anything like it and now it's a special favorite for us.

2 Ducks
1 orange, quartered
1 lemon, quartered
Salt & pepper
1/2 cup currant jelly
1/2 teaspoon lemon juice
1 tablespoon honey

1 can pitted black cherries
3/4 cup port wine
1 teaspoon lemon juice
1 tablespoon cornstarch
3 tablespoons sugar
2 tablespoons butter

Preheat oven to 375°.

Wash the ducks and pat dry. Sprinkle liberally with salt and pepper and stuff the cavities with the orange and lemon quarters. With a sharp knife or fork pierce the duck skin all over (pierce several more times during the roasting period). Roast for about 1 ½ hours. (The roasting time will depend on the size of your ducks).

Mix together currant jelly, lemon juice and honey and baste over the ducks using all of the mixture. Turn oven to 400 and roast for another 30 minutes.

For the sauce mix all of the ingredients in a medium saucepan and cook over medium heat until thickened, about 5 minutes. Pour some of the sauce over the ducks and serve some on the side. (You may want to double the sauce recipe.)

Baked Chicken and Rice

1 can cream mushroom soup
1 can water
3/4 cup long grain rice
Salt and pepper
4 chicken breasts or 6 thighs
Fresh parsley

Preheat oven to 375°.

In a shallow baking dish mix the soup water and rice. Place the chicken on top of this mixture and season with salt and pepper. Cover with foil and bake for 45 to 55 minutes

Remove and sprinkle with fresh parsley

Chicken and Potato Bake

When the cupboards are getting bare this makes a great supper. Super easy and only 3 ingredients.

1 chicken cut into serving pieces
2 cups Italian Salad Dressing
6 potatoes cut into chunks
2 large plastic zip lock bags

Preheat oven to 350°.

Put chicken pieces in one bag with 1 cup of the dressing. Put potatoes in the other bag with 1 cup of the dressing.

Refrigerate both and marinate for at least 2 hours. Remove chicken and potatoes, place in greased baking dish.

Bake uncovered for 1 ½ hours.

Grilled Barbeque Chicken

Chicken(s) for grilling
(You can either cut the chicken in pieces or just split it down the back)

Marinade:
1 cup Zesty Italian Salad Dressing
1/2 cup Olive Oil

Sauce:
3 tablespoons of butter
2 cloves of minced garlic
1 1/2 cups of catsup
1/4 cup of brown sugar
1/4 cup of cider vinegar
2 tablespoons of Worshtershire sauce
1 tablespoon of hot sauce (more if you like)
1 Bay Leaf
1 tablespoon of mustard

Wash and prepare chickens. Marinate the chicken in the marinade for at least 2 hours. Remove from marinade and sprinkle with salt and pepper.

Sauce Preparation:
Melt butter in saucepan and lightly sauté the garlic. Add all of the other ingredients and bring to a boil. Simmer for about 10 minutes and remove from heat.

Remove chicken from marinate and grill for 30 to 45 minutes depending on the size of your chicken. The last 15 minutes of grilling time baste the chicken with the sauce, turning occasionally.

Serve the extra sauce on the side.

Carolina CoCola Barbeque Sauce

2 tablespoons butter
1 medium onion, chopped fine
1 clove garlic, minced
2 bay leaves
2 1/2 cups catsup
8 ounces Coca Cola or Pepsi
1 1/2 tablespoons Worshtershire
2 teaspoons mustard
1 tablespoon apple cider vinegar

Melt the butter in a saucepan over low heat. Stir in the onion and cook until translucent.

Stir in all of the remaining ingredients.

Simmer over medium low heat for at least 30 minutes.

Bobby's Grilled Wings

20 to 25 chicken wings
1/4 cup hoisin sauce
1/2 cup olive oil
1 tablespoon soy sauce
1 tablespoon cider vinegar
3 or 4 tablespoons hot sauce
1 tablespoon freshly squeezed lemon juice
1 teaspoon light brown sugar
1 teaspoon chopped garlic
Salt and pepper

Put the wings in a large plastic zip top bag.

Combine all of the other ingredients and put ion the bag with the wings.

Refrigerate for at least 1 hour or overnight.

Prepare a charcoal or gas grill. Lightly spray the grill rack with vegetable-oil cooking spray.

Grill the wings, 25 to 30 minutes over a low heat until cooked through.

"Food is the most primitive form of comfort."

—Sheila Graham

Sweet and Sour Tropical Chicken

This is one of our favorite dishes for a family supper. This recipe is adapted from a Betty Crocker cookbook that I received at my wedding shower in 1978.

1 chicken cut up into serving pieces
1 cup flour
1 teaspoon salt
1 teaspoon pepper
1/3 cup oil for frying

Sauce:
1 20 ounce can sliced pineapple
1 cup sugar
2 tablespoons cornstarch
Water
3/4 cup cider vinegar
1 tablespoon soy sauce
1/4 teaspoon ginger
1 chicken bouillon cube
1 large green pepper sliced

Pre-heat oven to 350°.

Sprinkle the chicken with the salt and pepper and then dredge in the flour. In a fry pan, heat the oil to medium high and brown the chicken on all sides. Place browned chicken in a two quart casserole dish.

Make Sauce:
Drain the juice from the pineapple into a 2 cup measure. Add water to make 1 ¼ cups. Pour this mixture into a medium saucepan, stir in the sugar and the cornstarch and bring to a boil. Add the vinegar, ginger, and the bouillon cube. Pour

this mixture over the chicken. Cut the pineapple into bite size pieces and place on top of chicken along with the bell pepper slices. Cover and bake for 1 ½ hours.

Chicken Casserole

1 large chicken cooked and de-boned
1 package Pepperidge Farm Stuffing Mix
1 stick butter, melted
1 can cream chicken soup
1 (8ounce) container sour cream
1 can chicken broth

Preheat oven to 350°.

Mix the cream of chicken soup, sour cream and chicken broth together until smooth.

In a greased casserole dish start making layers of stuffing mix, chicken and soup mix. Repeat the layers until all ingredients are used. End with a little of the stuffing mix and pour the melted butter over the top.

Bake for 35 to 40 minutes

Barbecued Doves

Doves
Bacon
Toothpicks
Italian Salad Dressing
Your Favorite Barbecue Sauce

Clean the doves and pop out the breasts (make sure you get any bird shot out)

Wrap the breast in bacon and secure it with a toothpick. (you don't have to use a whole slice, a half slice should go around a breast)

Put them in a pan and pour Italian Dressing over the top.

Marinate overnight or for at least 2 hours.

Grill the doves, basting frequently with the barbecue sauce until the bacon is done. Depending on the size of your birds you should only need to grill them for 5 to 10 minutes.

Note from Vicki

The only kind of hunting my husband does is for birds, and usually just for doves. (Now fishing is another story!) We went to a friend's house about 15 years ago who is an avid hunter and he served us Barbeque Dove. We loved it and decided that we like them better this way than in a stew with gravy. A dove has a tendency to be on the dry side so be careful not to overcook.

Perfect Prime Rib

Don't be afraid to try this. Everyone is always afraid they will mess up that expensive piece of meat, but you really can't go wrong. Just salt, pepper and heat, that's all it takes.

1 rib eye loin
Kosher salt
Freshly cracked black pepper

Remove the roast from the refrigerator at least an hour before cooking. It should be at room temperature before you start the cooking process.

Preheat your oven to 475° to 500°. Make sure you have a really clean oven or you are going to have a smoke filled kitchen.

Generously rub salt and pepper on all sides of the roast. Place the roast, fat side up in a roasting pan.

Cook for 15 minutes on the high heat and then reduce the temperature to 350.

You should allow about 15 minutes per pound for rare (which is how I like it). If you like it medium rare cook about 20 minutes per pound and if you like it well done ..., well you should just go get a hamburger.

If you want to use a meat thermometer for rare it should read 120° and for medium rare 135°.

Remove from the oven and let stand at least 15 minutes. The meat will continue to cook after you have removed it from the oven so when I think it's "just about" where I want it, I take it out.

The Best Hamburgers

1 1/2 pounds hamburger (80/20)
1 stick cold butter cut into pieces
3/4 cup water
1 teaspoon salt
1 teaspoon black pepper

Mix all ingredients together and pat out four burgers.

Grill or cook in cast iron skillet until done to your liking. (I like mine medium to medium rare.)

Serve on hamburger buns with your favorite condiments.

These burgers are great after a hard day of fishing.

"Some people never miss a good chance to shut up."

—Southern Saying

Spaghetti Carbonara

This is a very easy and quick recipe and can be halved easily. You usually have all of the ingredients in your house anyway so it's a good dish to make when the cupboards are low. Plus what's not to like.... bacon, egg, and cheese.

1 pound spaghetti (cooked)
2 pounds bacon, chopped
1 tablespoon chopped garlic
Freshly ground black pepper
4 large eggs, beaten
1 cup freshly grated Parmesan cheese
2 tablespoons finely chopped fresh parsley leaves

In a large sauté pan cook the bacon until crispy.

Remove the bacon and drain on paper towels. Pour off all of the oil except for 4 tablespoons.

Add the garlic.

Add the crispy bacon and the cooked pasta. Sauté for 1 minute.

Beat the eggs together with the cheese until smooth.

Remove the pan from the heat and add the egg and cheese mixture, whisking quickly until the eggs thicken, but do not scramble. Season with salt and pepper.

Sprinkle with parsley.

Note from Vicki

When cooking pasta do not add any oil to the water. Your sauce will not stick to the pasta if you do.

Stuffed Shells

1 (16 ounce) package jumbo pasta shells
1/2 pound Italian sausage
1 (10 ounce) package frozen chopped spinach—thawed, drained and squeezed dry
1 cup ricotta cheese
1 egg
3 cloves crushed garlic
Juice from one lemon
1/2 cup grated Parmesan cheese
Salt and pepper to taste
2 cups marinara sauce
2 cups shredded mozzarella cheese
Fresh basil leaves

Preheat oven to 350°.

Add about 1 tablespoon of salt to a large pot of water. Bring to a boil. Add shells and cook for 8 to 10 minutes or until al dente; drain and rinse in cold water.

Brown sausage in a large skillet until done. Drain off all of the grease and crumble the sausage.

In a large bowl, combine the sausage, spinach, ricotta cheese, egg, garlic, lemon juice and Parmesan cheese. Season with salt and pepper.

Stuff pasta shells with the sausage and cheese mixture and place in a 9x13 inch baking dish.

Top with marinara sauce, mozzarella cheese, torn basil leaves, and bake for 30 minutes.

Boiled Smoked Picnic
with Great Northern's

A picnic is the shoulder of a pig. This cut has more fat in it than the "ham", which comes from the hind legs, and we all know that fat equals flavor. A picnic is also a cheaper cut of meat and very economical. It's great for sandwiches too.

Take one smoked picnic and put in a large pot. Put in enough water so that it covers the top of the picnic.

Bring the water to a boil and then turn down to a slow simmer.

Simmer the picnic for 1 hour. Remove from water and put onto a serving platter.

Wash one package of great northern beans and put the beans in the pot with the water the ham was cooked in.

Cut up one small onion and add to the pot. Cover and simmer for 2 hours.

You can eat off of this meal for almost a whole week.

Southern Baked Ham

This is a staple at all southern holiday meals, especially Easter.

1 fresh (not smoked) ham about 12 to 15 pounds
2 cans Coca Cola or Pepsi
Whole Cloves
1 can pineapple slices (reserve juice)
1 cup brown sugar
1/2 cup honey
1/2 cup reserved pineapple juice
2 tablespoons flour
1 teaspoon dry mustard
2 tablespoons vinegar

Preheat oven to 350°.

Score ham in diagonally in a crisscross fashion with knife. Stick whole cloves into ham where lines cross. Pour 1 can of the cola over the ham, cover with foil and bake 1 hour. Remove from oven and pour the other can of soda over the ham. Cover and continue to cook for another 1 ½ hours.

Turn oven to 400°.

With toothpicks stick pineapple slices over top and sides of ham.

Mix the remaining ingredients together.

Pour about ½ of this mixture over the ham and wrap tightly in aluminum foil and cook for 1 hour.

Uncover ham and pour the remaining sugar mixture over the ham.

Bake uncovered for 30 more minutes.

Grilled Pork Tenderloin

These always turn out juicy and tender.

1 or 2 Pork Tenderloins

Marinade:
1 clove of garlic, minced
3/4 cup olive oil
2 tablespoons Soy Sauce
2 tablespoons Balsamic Vinegar
3 tablespoons Apple juice
1 tablespoon hot sauce
1 tablespoon hoisen sauce

Combine all of the marinade ingredients and stir to combine.

Place the pork tenderloin in a plastic, sealable bag. Pour marinade over the tenderloin and marinate overnight in the refrigerator.

Preheat an outdoor grill for medium heat.

Remove pork from marinade and pat dry.

Grill tenderloin until cooked through, about 25 minutes.

Remove from heat and allow to rest for at least 15 minutes. Slice and enjoy.

Note from Vicki

Be careful not to overcook this. People have a tendency to overcook pork and if you do it will be dry and tough. It's okay if it's a tad pink. Use a meat thermometer and remove it from the oven when it reads about 138-140 degrees. The pork will continue to "cook" as it rests and the temperature will rise up to another 6 to 8 degrees.

Neck Bones and Rice

My Grandma Lotha used to make this a lot. Yes its cheap eatin', but there's nothing that says cheap can't be good.

2 1/2 to 3 pounds of fresh pork neck bones (not smoked or cured)
enough oil to just cover the bottom of a heavy stew pot or cast iron pot
2 teaspoons salt
1 teaspoon pepper
6 cups of water
1 medium onion, diced
2 cups rice

Put your pot on the fire and add the oil.

Brown the neck bones really good on all sides (Get a lot of color in the bottom of the pot, that's all flavor!)

Add the onions and cook until transparent.

Pour in the water, salt and pepper and bring to boil.

Cover the pot and simmer on low for 1½ to 2 hours.

Add the rice.

Cover and simmer for about 20 more minutes or until rice is done.

Grilled Pork Chops

1/2 cup chopped fresh parsley
1/4 cup chopped fresh basil
2 garlic cloves, minced
1/4 cup balsamic vinegar
3/4 cup olive oil
1 tablespoon soy sauce
8 (8-ounce) pork chops

Combine first 6 ingredients in zip-top plastic bag; add pork chops. Seal and chill 4 to 6 hours.

Remove chops from marinade.

Grill over medium-high heat 6 to 8 minutes on each side or until done.

Hashlet Stew (Haslet)
Pork Stew

4 to 5 pieces of Salt Pork (Fat back)
1 pound of country style pork ribs cut into pieces
1 pound of pork spare ribs cut into pieces
Pork liver, lites, heart (or whatever pork meat you can get)
2 medium onions chopped
2 cloves garlic
1 stick butter
3 tablespoons flour
Water
Salt and pepper
1 tablespoon of hot sauce
1 tablespoon of Worshtershire Sauce
1 tablespoon A-1 Steak Sauce™
1 Bay leaf
OPTIONAL: Cornmeal dumplings

(You can add any other fresh pork meat you can get your hands on. Do not use any smoked meat, only fresh meat, and no sausage.)

(For parts like the liver and heart, boil first, then dice in chunks and brown)

In a large stew pot fry the salt pork until fat is rendered out.

Salt and Pepper the pork and add the meat a little at a time and brown well. You might have to remove some of the meat and do this in stages to get the meat really browned.

Remove meat and add onions to the pot with 1 stick of butter.

Cook onions and garlic until soft.

Add flour and cook until a light golden color.

Return all of the meat to the pot and add water to barely cover.

Add Bay leaf and cut up potatoes

Stir well to mix all ingredients and simmer on low for 45 minutes to an hour.

OPTIONAL: (The last 20 minutes you may add cornmeal dumplings to the liquid)

Note from Vicki

Hashlet Stew, as we call it, is something that originated at Hog Killin' time. You don't see it, or hear about it too much anymore, because the parts that were originally used to make the stew are no longer readily available. The original recipe calls for the lites (lungs), liver, and heart of the pig. The official meaning of the word haslet is: *The heart, liver, and other edible viscera of an animal, especially hog viscera. The soft internal organs of the body, especially those contained within the abdominal and thoracic cavities.* So a little bit of everything went in here. Nothing went to waste.

Mr. Smith Dowty and unknown friend, busy at a hog killin'.

I believe that the sale of lites was banned sometime back in the sixty's. Of course if you know someone that still kills their own hogs you can make the original version and some of the butcher shops or pork stores may have some of the ingredients you need.

Great-Grandmama Margie making sausage at a Hog Killin' in
Grandmama Velma's back yard.

Bobby's mother made this stew a lot and it is one of his favorites. My Grandma
Velma used to make it for him at Christmas or Thanksgiving and now it has
fallen to me to keep up the tradition. Of course I can't use that original version
because you just have a really hard time getting the stuff and we don't kill our
own hogs.... so get the different kind of pork meats that you can and give it a try.

Sweet Endings

Cakes & Frostings

As they say,
"We save the best for last"
Sweet Desserts,
Cakes, Pies, Cookies, and Candy
Yum!

"Seize the moment. Remember all those women on the 'Titanic' who waved off the dessert cart."

—Erma Bombeck

Don't be afraid to attempt something you've never done before. And that goes for everything, not just cooking. Life is too short!! I had never made a wedding cake before, or for that matter any kind of piped decorated cake, but I had always wanted to. I had planned to make my daughter Brandi's cake for her wedding, but all of my friends and family talked me out of it, saying I would be too stressed and I had too many other things to do (I still think I could have managed). When my niece Michelle's wedding came around here was my chance. I had a great time making this cake. I rolled fondant pearls every night for about a month and threw away more handmade flowers than I ended up with, but it was still fun and the bride loved it.

Michelle and Lance Shields'—Wedding Cake

Velma's Pecan & Raisin Cake

I have never known anyone who makes this cake except my grandmother. She taught me how to make this simple cake and I have never had it anywhere else. We always have this cake at Thanksgiving and Christmas and any special occasion. Just looking at the recipe you would not think that it would taste that special, but take my word for it, it does. My grandmother says that it's better if you make it a day ahead and put it in an airtight container in the refrigerator. This cake is a big part of my life and our family traditions. I can't even begin to think about a holiday without it, and to me it will always be "Grandmama's Cake". (I have copied this down exactly as she wrote it.)

1 box of German Chocolate Cake mix

Make cake in 4 layers according to the directions on the package. Cool the layers completely, or even better, cool them, freeze them, and put the cake together the next day.

1 pint of whipping cream
1/2 box of powdered sugar
1 teaspoon vanilla
1/2 box of raisins
2 cups chopped pecans

Whip the cream until fluffy and thick (but not until it turns to butter).

Add the sugar and flavoring and mix well.

Spread the whipped cream mixture on the layers and drop on raisins and pecans. Do this for all layers.

Frost the top and sides. Decorate the top with some whole pecans and a few raisins. Add a few candied cherries for decoration.

The Cheesecake

This cheesecake is really special. I only make it once or twice a year, for some-one's birthday or if we are all on a family vacation at the beach for a week. It's really rich and creamy and the best cheesecake I've ever had.

Crust:

1 1/4 cups vanilla wafer crumbs	6 tablespoons butter
1/2 cup ground pecans (optional)	1 tablespoon sugar

Preheat oven to 375°.

Melt the butter, mix with remaining ingredients and press into the bottom of a 10 inch spring form pan. Bake for 15 minutes. Remove from oven and set aside to cool.

REDUCE OVEN TEMPERATURE TO 300°.
Put a pan of hot water on the bottom rack of the oven.

Filling:

6 8 ounce packages of cream cheese	1 cups sugar
3 large whole eggs	2 teaspoons vanilla
2 egg whites, beaten until firm	1 tablespoon flour
1 tablespoon lemon juice	

Beat the cream cheese, sugar and vanilla until fluffy and smooth. Add the 3 whole eggs, the 2 egg yolks, the flour, and beat well. Blend in the vanilla and lemon juice.

Fold the beaten egg whites into the cheese mixture. Pour the mixture over the crust in the spring form pan.

Bake on the center rack of the oven for 1 hour. TURN OFF OVEN. Remove the cake after an additional ½ hour

Refrigerate cake. When cold serve topped with your favorite fruit. (Sweetened strawberries are great with this.)

Chocolate Chip Cheesecake

Use the same filling and the same baking directions as for "The Cheesecake"

For the crust press one roll of refrigerated chocolate chip cookie dough into the bottom of the spring form pan. Do not pre-bake.

For the filling, add 1/3 cup of chocolate chips to the batter.

Bake following the same directions as "The Cheesecake". (300 degrees)

When cheesecake is cool, melt ¾ cup of chocolate chips with 2 tablespoons of heavy cream.

Pour the chocolate over the top of the cake and return to the refrigerator to set.

Chocolate Chocolate Cake

1 3/4 cups flour

2 cups sugar

3/4 cup cocoa

1 1/2 teaspoons baking soda

1 1/2 teaspoons baking powder

Pinch of salt

2 eggs

1 cup whole milk

1/2 cup oil

2 teaspoons vanilla

1 cup boiling water

Preheat oven to 350°. Mix all of the dry ingredients together in a bowl.

In another bowl mix the eggs, milk, oil and vanilla. Add this mixture to the dry ingredients and blend well. Stir in the boiling water to the batter. Pour batter into 2 or 3 greased and floured (see note) round baking pans.

Bake for 25 to 30 minutes or until a toothpick inserted in the center comes out clean. Remove from pans and cool.

<u>Frosting</u>

1/2 cup butter

2/3 cup cocoa

4 1/2 cups powdered sugar

1/3 to 1/2 cup half and half

1 teaspoon vanilla

pinch of salt

In large saucepan, melt together butter and cocoa.

Using mixer, alternately beat in powdered sugar and milk until frosting is smooth and creamy. Stir in vanilla and salt. Frost and fill the layers.

Chocolate Pecan Cream Cake

This was Bobby's Birthday cake for his 60th birthday. This keeps really well and is always moist.

1 recipe for Classic Yellow Cake Layers
1 recipe for Classic Chocolate Frosting
1 recipe for Classic Vanilla Cream Filling
1 1/2 cups of chopped pecans

Cool the cake layers completely or make them the day before and freeze.

Split the layers and spread the vanilla cream in between.

Frost with Classic Chocolate frosting.

Press chopped pecans into the sides of the frosted cake all the way around.

Decorate the top with whole pecans.

HoHo Cake

I always make this cake for my friend Linda's birthday. It's a really good cake that has a creamy white filling and chocolate frosting.

Cake:

1 Devils Food Cake Mix

(Mix according to directions)

 teaspoon vanilla flavoring

1 teaspoon butter flavoring

1 tablespoon cocoa

Bake in three pans according to directions on box. Remove from pans and put in freezer for at least 2 hours. (I usually make the layers the day before and freeze.)

Filling:

5 tablespoons flour

1 1/4 cups milk

1 cup sugar

1 small jar Marshmallow Fluff

1/2 cup butter

1 teaspoon vanilla

1/2 cup Crisco shortening

Mix the flour and the milk together over medium heat until smooth and thick. Refrigerate until COLD. In a stand mixer blend the Crisco, butter, sugar and vanilla until smooth and no longer grainy (about 5 minutes). Add in the marshmallow and blend another 2 to 3 minutes. Spread this mixture between the cake layers.

Frosting:

1/2 cup butter

2/3 cup HERSHEY'S Cocoa

1 teaspoon vanilla

3 cups powdered sugar

1/3 cup milk

Melt butter. Stir in cocoa. Alternately add powdered sugar and milk, beating to spreading consistency. Add small amount additional milk, if needed. Stir in vanilla. Frost top and sides of cake.

Mama's Fudge Cake

Mama gave me this recipe about ten years ago and it has been one of my family's favorites ever since. This cake keeps really well. Great for a picnic or trip to the beach. It also happens to be Bobby's favorite cake.

Cake:

2 sticks butter

1 cup water

3 tablespoons cocoa

2 cups sugar

2 cups flour

2 eggs

1 teaspoon vanilla

1/2 cup buttermilk

Topping:

1 stick butter

3 tablespoons cocoa

6 tablespoons milk

1 teaspoon vanilla

1 box powdered sugar

1 1/2 cups chopped pecans

Preheat oven to 350°.

In a saucepan bring the butter, water and cocoa to a boil.

In a mixing bowl put in the flour and sugar and pour in the chocolate mixture.

Blend well and add in the eggs vanilla and buttermilk. Mix until smooth.

Pour into 9 x 13 pan and bake for 30 minutes (do not over bake).

For the topping in a saucepan bring to a boil the butter cocoa and milk. Stir in the powdered sugar, vanilla and pecans.

Pour the warm mixture over warm cake.

Old Fashioned Coconut Cake

All of my grandmothers' made this cake. An old fashioned coconut cake, that's another southern staple.

Cake:

6 large eggs, separated

3/4 cup butter

1 1/2 cups sugar

2 1/2 cups all purpose flour

2 teaspoons baking powder

1/2 teaspoon baking soda

1/2 teaspoon salt

1 1/2 cups buttermilk

1 teaspoon vanilla extract

Frosting and Filling:

2 egg whites

1-1/2 cups sugar

5 Tbsp water

2 cups of sweetened flaked coconut

1/4 teaspoon cream of tartar

1-1/2 tsp light corn syrup

1 tsp vanilla extract

Preheat oven to 350°

For the cake: Blend the 6 egg yolks together with the butter and sugar until smooth and creamy. Combine the dry ingredients and blend into to sugar and egg mixture alternately with the buttermilk. When blended well add in the vanilla. Pour into 4 greased and floured pans and bake for 25 minutes or until toothpick inserted in the center comes out clean. Cool the layers completely.

For the icing and filling: Combine all ingredients except the vanilla in the top of a double boiler. Mix until thoroughly blended and place over rapidly boiling water and beat with a hand mixer for 7 minutes. Add the vanilla and continue beating until the icing reaches a good consistency for spreading. Spread icing on cake layer and sprinkle with coconut. Continue until all layers are done then spread icing on the top and sides and cover with the coconut.

Note from Vicki

Make sure you use sweetened flaked coconut in the bag for this recipe. The frozen coconut will not work the same.

Velvety Candy Bar Cake

I made this cake for an old friend and her husband. Now every time I see them they still talk about this cake.

Cake:
1 (18.25 ounce) package devil's food cake mix
1 1/2 cups milk
3 eggs
3/4 cup vegetable oil
1 (3.5 ounce) package instant vanilla pudding mix

Frosting:
1 (8 ounce) package cream cheese
1/2 cup sugar
1 cup powdered sugar
1 teaspoon vanilla
1 (12 ounce) container frozen whipped topping, thawed
1 cup chopped pecans
4 (1.5 ounce) bars milk chocolate candy with almonds, chopped

Cake:
Preheat oven to 325°. Grease and flour 3 cake pans.

In a large bowl, combine cake mix, milk, eggs, oil and instant vanilla pudding mix. Beat on low speed until well blended. Pour batter into prepared pans.

Bake for 20 to 25 minutes, or until a toothpick inserted into the center of the cake comes out clean. Allow to cool completely.

Frosting:

In a large bowl, beat the cream cheese, sugar, vanilla and powdered sugar until smooth. Fold in the whipped topping, pecans and chopped candy bars. Spread between layers and on top and sides of cake.

Coca-Cola Cake with Frosting

Another old recipe. I think this was made a lot in the 60's. It's a really good chocolate cake.

Cake:
2 cups sugar
2 cups AP flour
1 1/2 cups of mini marshmallows
1/2 cup butter
1/2 cup vegetable oil
3 tablespoons of cocoa
1 cup Coca-Cola (or as we say co-cola)
1/2 cup buttermilk
1 teaspoon baking soda
1 teaspoon vanilla

Preheat oven to 350º. Mix together sugar and flour; add marshmallows. Set aside.

In medium saucepan, over medium heat, add butter, oil, cocoa, and Coca-Cola and bring to a boil. Remove from heat. Pour over dry ingredients and blend well. Add buttermilk, baking soda, eggs, and vanilla. Mix well and pour into greased 9x13 baking pan. Bake for 45 minutes. Remove from oven and frost immediately.

Frosting:
1/2 cup butter
3 tablespoons cocoa
6 tablespoons Coca-Cola
1 pound of powdered sugar
1 teaspoon vanilla
1 cup chopped pecans

In saucepan, over medium heat, combine butter, cocoa, and Coco-Cola. Bring to a boil and add sugar. Remove from heat. Add vanilla and pecans. Frost Cake.

Yellow Cake Layers

This cake is good for birthday cakes and great with chocolate icing. Experiment with different fillings and frostings.

1/2 cup butter, softened

1 1/4 cups sugar

2 eggs

3/4 cup milk

1 teaspoon vanilla extract

1 teaspoon butter flavoring

2 cups AP flour

1 tablespoon baking powder

1 teaspoon salt

Preheat oven to 375°.

In a stand mixer blend the butter with the sugar until well blended. Add the eggs, the milk and the flavorings.

In a separate bowl mix all of the dry ingredients together. Slowly blend the dry ingredients with the wet. Do not over beat.

Bake in greased and floured pans (or 13 x 9 pan) for 25 to 30 minutes or until a toothpick inserted in the center comes out clean.

Quick Yellow Cake Layers

When you don't have the time or ingredients to make layers from scratch, try this.

1 box butter cake mix

1 1/3 cups buttermilk

4 eggs

1/2 cup sugar

1/2cup Wesson oil

Preheat oven to 350°. Mix ingredients thoroughly. Bake for 30 to 35 minutes. Makes 3, 8 inch layers

Vanilla Cream Filling

2 tablespoons cornstarch

1 cup half and half

1/4 cup sugar

1 tablespoon butter

1 teaspoon vanilla

1 pinch salt

1 egg

In a saucepan mix the cornstarch, half and half and sugar together. Cook over medium heat until it comes to a boil and thickens. Remove from heat and add eggs. Return to heat and cook another 2 to 3 minutes. This mixture will be thick and smooth. Remove from heat and add vanilla and butter. Let cool completely.

Caramel Icing

1 1/4 cups brown sugar

2 egg whites

1/4 teaspoon cream of tartar

1 teaspoon vanilla

5 tablespoons water

Pinch of salt

Put all of the ingredients in the top of a double boiler with water boiling. Beat with an electric mixer for 7 minutes or until soft peaks form.

Seven-Minute Icing

2 egg whites

1-1/2 cups sugar

5 Tbsp water

1/4 teaspoon cream of tartar

1-1/2 tsp light corn syrup

1 tsp vanilla extract

Combine all ingredients except the vanilla in the top of a double boiler (not on the heat yet). Mix until thoroughly blended and place over rapidly boiling water and beat with a hand mixer for 7 minutes. Add the vanilla and continue beating until the icing reaches a good consistency for spreading.

Unbelievably Easy Chocolate Frosting

1 1/2 ounces of unsweetened chocolate squares (melted)
1/4 cup of evaporated milk (NOT condensed milk)
1/2 cup of sugar

Add milk to blender, turn on and add the melted chocolate and sugar. Blend until the mixture is thick.

NOTE: You must have a blender or this will not work!

Elegant Cream Cheese Frosting

8 oz cream cheese softened
2 tablespoons of butter
2 teaspoons of milk or cream
1 teaspoon of vanilla
3 to 4 cups of powdered sugar (depending on how thick you want the icing)

Mix together cream cheese and butter until smooth. Add vanilla and 2 teaspoons of milk. Slowly blend in powdered sugar to the desired consistency.

Unforgettable Marshmallow Frosting

1 cup Marshmallow Fluff

2 egg whites

1 cup of sugar

1/4 teaspoon cream of tartar

1/8 teaspoon salt

1/4 cup water

1 teaspoon vanilla

In a double boiler combine all of the ingredients except the vanilla. Beat with a hand mixer until soft peaks form. Remove from the heat and continue to beat until the mixture is stiff. Stir in vanilla.

Pig Pickin' Cake

This was my Daddy's favorite cake. It's so easy and so good. I usually make my layers a day ahead (or at least a few hours ahead) and put them in the freezer. The cake will stay together and frost a lot easier if you do it that way. I also think that freezing the layers makes the cake moist.

1 yellow cake mix
2 1-ounce cans mandarin oranges (do not drain one can)
4 eggs
1/2 cup vegetable oil
1 teaspoon butter flavoring
1 teaspoon vanilla
9-ounce carton frozen whipped topping, thawed
    (I use the extra creamy non-dairy whipped topping)
1 12-ounce can crushed pineapple in heavy syrup
1 small can crushed pineapple (to put on top of cake)
2 small boxes instant vanilla pudding

Preheat oven to 350°. Grease and flour three 9-inch cake pans.

In mixing bowl, combine cake mix, 1 can of the mandarin oranges with the juice, eggs and oil.

Beat for 2 minutes with electric mixer. Pour into pans and bake for 20 to 25 minutes or until cake tester comes out clean. Cool cake on racks.

In a mixing bowl, combine whipped topping, pineapple, juice from can and vanilla pudding mix.

Fill and frost the cake with this mixture. Decorate with remaining can of oranges and small can of pineapple.

"Grandmama's Cake"

I was halfway there and the smell of it hit me square in the face. The corners of my mouth turned upward and the smile would still be visible when I walked through her door. She knew that I would come for my daily visit as soon as the school bus dropped me off at our house just down the road and she thought she would make my day a little brighter by baking the pineapple cake that was my absolute favorite. She was just putting the finishing touches on. Getting the creamy icing, full of yellow crushed pineapple, all over the top and all around the sides. It stayed in place perfectly.

I looked up at her and smiled. I didn't ask the question she knew was utmost on my mind, I just sat down at the yellow and green kitchen table and my sweaty legs stuck to the plastic seats of the chair. "And how was your day today" she asked? "Anything interesting happen at school?" "Nope," I answered with my hands propped under my chin and my eyes still on the cake.

She went to the old refrigerator and pulled out a pitcher of cold milk and poured a glass. She sat it down on the table in front of me. "Thanks Grandma." I studied the little pale yellow creamy bits of cream floating on top of the milk and out of the corner of my eye I saw her go get a saucer from the pie safe where she kept her dishes. She took it over to the pineapple cake and reached behind her to the drawer beside the sink to get her big cutting knife that she used for everything from cutting up chicken to slicing cake. She cut a big wedge and put it in the saucer and walked back over to the refrigerator. The pint jar she retrieved was filled with that same pale yellow cream that floated on top of the milk. She opened the jar, grabbed a tablespoon and put a big dollop of the thick cream on top of the cake. She looked at me and smiled and slid the saucer over to me.

She always did know how to make my day a little brighter.

Luscious Lemon Cream Cake

The Cake:

1 cup room temperature butter

2 cups sugar

3 eggs

1 teaspoon vanilla flavoring

1 teaspoon butter flavoring

Grated rind from one lemon

3 1/2 cups cake flour

2 teaspoons baking powder

1 teaspoon baking soda

Pinch of salt

2 cups sour cream

Preheat oven to 350°. Grease the bottom of 3 (8 or 9 inch) round cake pans.

Cream butter and sugar together and add eggs one at a time. Add the flavorings and lemon peel. Sift dry ingredients together and add to creamed mixture alternately with sour cream.

Divide batter among three pans. Bake for 30-35 minutes or until tests done. Cool the layers completely or freeze for later assembly.

The Filling and Frosting:
1 package lemon pudding/pie filling (not instant)
1/3 cup sugar
2 eggs
2 cups milk
1 cup of heavy whipping cream
1 teaspoon grated lemon peel

Combine pudding mix, sugar and eggs in saucepan. Add milk and cook over medium heat, stirring constantly. Bring to boil, reduce heat and cook 5 minutes. Remove from heat, add the grated lemon peel and cool completely.

Whip the heavy cream until soft peaks form and then combine with the lemon mixture. Put filling between the layers of cake and frost sides and top.

Boston Cream Cake

My Grandma Lotha made Boston Cream Pie all the time. I loved the creamy middle and the dark chocolate.

Cake Part	Cream Part
1/3 cup butter	2 tablespoons cornstarch
3/4 cup sugar	1 cup half and half
1 teaspoon vanilla	1/4 cup of sugar
2 large eggs	1 egg
1 1/2 cups all purpose flour	1 teaspoon vanilla
2 tsp. baking powder	1 pinch of salt
1/2 teaspoon salt	1 tablespoon of butter
1/2 cup milk	

Chocolate Glaze Part
4 oz. semi-sweet chocolate
2 tablespoons butter

Preheat oven to 375° and grease and flour 2 cake pans.

Make Cake:
In mixer bowl cream the butter, sugar and vanilla until creamy and then add the eggs one at a time. Fold in flour and other dry ingredients, add milk and mix until well blended. Pour into pans and bake until toothpick inserted in the center comes out clean. Remove cake from pans and set aside to cool. (You can also make these layers ahead of time and freeze.)

Make Cream Filling:

In a saucepan mix the cornstarch, half and half and sugar together. Cook over medium heat until it comes to a boil and thickens. Remove from heat and add eggs. Return to heat and cook another 2 to 3 minutes. This mixture will be thick and smooth. Remove from heat and add vanilla and butter. Let cool completely.

Make Glaze:

In a heavy saucepan, melt chocolate and butter over low heat; stir until smooth. Spread glaze over top of cake.

Refrigerate until ready to serve.

Miss Alice's Red Velvet Cake

My Grandmama always used Miss Alice's recipe when she made a Red Velvet Cake. Sometimes she would double the icing recipe. Miss Alice was married to my Granddaddy's first cousin.

3 eggs	1/4 teaspoon baking powder
2 cups sugar	1 1/2 teaspoons baking soda
1 cup buttermilk	1 teaspoon vanilla
2 1/2 to 3 cups flour	1 tablespoon cocoa
1/2 cup butter	1 tablespoon vinegar
1/2 teaspoon salt	2 ounces of red food coloring

Cake Layers:
Preheat oven to 350°
Cream the butter and the sugar. Add eggs one at a time and beat until fluffy. Make a paste of the vinegar and cocoa and add to the sugar mixture. Add the dry ingredients to the mixture alternately with the buttermilk. Stir in the vanilla and the food coloring. Pour into 2 or 3 greased pan and bake for 25 minutes or until done.

Filling & Icing

1 can evaporated milk	1 teaspoon vanilla
3 sticks butter, whipped	1 cup chopped pecans
1 cup sugar	1 can coconut
2 tablespoons flour	

In a saucepan mix the milk and the flour and on low heat cook until thickened. Let this mixture cool completely. Cream the sugar and the butter together until smooth and then add in the flour mixture. Beat this mixture until it looks like whipped cream. Add the pecans, coconut and vanilla. Blend Well.

Spread this between the layers and on the sides and top of the cake.

Cream Cheese Pound Cake

I've made lots of different pound cakes seeing if there was possibly one that is better than this but the search is over. This is the perfect pound cake.

Note from Vicki

Make sure you don't over bake this cake and make sure you use big eggs (I use Jumbo or extra large. If your eggs are small add one or two more).

3 cups sugar
3 sticks butter
1 package of cream cheese
6 eggs
3 cups AP Flour
2 teaspoons vanilla
1/4 teaspoon of salt

Preheat oven to 325°

Blend butter, sugar and cream cheese until smooth.

Add eggs one at a time, mixing well after each addition.

Add flour and mix until all flour is incorporated (do not over mix). Stir in salt and vanilla.

Pour mixture into well greased and floured bundt pan or tube pan. Bake 325 degrees for 50-60 minutes.

VARIATIONS

Chocolate Marble Pound Cake—Take half of the batter and mix with 3 tablespoons of cocoa powder and ¼ cup of milk. Put half of the yellow mixture in the pan and put half of the chocolate on the other side of the pan. Dollop the remaining yellow on top of the chocolate and the remaining chocolate on top of the yellow.

Sweet
Endings

Pies, Desserts, Cookies
&
Confections

"Good apple pies are a considerable part of our domestic happiness."

—Jane Austen

Never Fail Meringue

I use this meringue recipe to top all of the custard pies that I make.

1 tablespoon cornstarch
2 tablespoons cold water
1/2 cup boiling water
1 teaspoon vanilla extract
4 egg whites
1/2 teaspoon cream of tartar
6 tablespoons white sugar
1 pinch salt

Blend the cornstarch and cold water in a saucepan. Add the boiling water, and cook until thick and clear. Cool completely. (Put in the refrigerator for at least 30 minutes).

Beat egg whites with the cream of tartar until foamy. Gradually beat in sugar, beating until stiff and glossy. Add the salt and vanilla, and slowly beat in cold cornstarch mixture.

Beat until stiff peaks form. Spread meringue on filled pie shell making sure to touch the edge of the pie shell all the way around.

Bake at 350° for 8 to 10 minutes.

Scrumptious Lemon Pie

Lemon pie was once a staple at every seafood restaurant you visited. I guess folks have fallen out of favor with pie. Those fancy towering desserts have taken over. Well believe me, after a meal of seafood there is nothing better in the world than lemon pie. It's just a natural.

1 1/2 cups sugar
6 tablespoons cornstarch
2 cups water
1/3 cup fresh lemon juice
1 teaspoon fresh grated lemon zest
3 eggs—separated
3 tablespoons butter
1 teaspoon lemon extract

Mix the cornstarch and sugar together in a saucepan.

In a 4 cup measure add the water, lemon juice and egg yolks, reserving the whites for meringue.

Add this mixture to the sugar and cornstarch and cook over medium heat stirring constantly until thick.

Remove from heat and add the butter and flavoring.

Pour into pre-baked pie shell.

Top with "Never Fail Meringue" and bake in 350° oven until golden

Grandmama Velma's Famous Coconut Cream Pie

My grandma Velma is famous for this coconut cream pie. She gave me this recipe when we owned a restaurant and this was one of our most requested desserts.

1 baked pie crust
3 egg yolks
1 cup sugar
Pinch of salt
1 cup whole milk
1/2 cup canned milk
3 heaping tablespoons flour
1 cup fresh ground coconut
1 teaspoon vanilla
1 tablespoon butter

Separate the eggs and put whites in a bowl to make meringue

In a saucepan mix the sugar, salt, milk and flour. Cook over medium heat until slightly thickened

Beat egg yolks and temper with some of the hot mixture and quickly add all back to saucepan, stirring constantly. Add in the coconut and simmer for another two minutes.

Remove from heat and stir in the vanilla and butter.

Pour into pre-baked pie shell.

Top with "Never Fail Meringue" and bake in 350° oven until golden

Butterscotch Pie

My Grandma Velma used to make this butterscotch pie and it was my absolute favorite dessert. Then suddenly for some reason she stopped making it. I didn't realize how much I had been missing it until I ran across this recipe in her kitchen recently.

1 cup brown sugar
1/4 cup granulated white sugar
4 tablespoons flour
Pinch of salt
1 cup evaporated canned milk
3/4 cup of whole milk
3 egg yolks
1 teaspoon vanilla
2 tablespoons butter

In a saucepan mix the sugars, salt, and the flour together. Over medium heat slowly add the milks. Cook until it begins to thicken.

Add a little of the cooked mixture to 3 beaten egg yolks and return to the saucepan stirring constantly.

Remove from heat and add the vanilla and the butter. Cool slightly and pour into prepared crust.

Top with "Never Fail Meringue" and bake in 350° oven for 8 to 10 minutes.

Grandmama Margie's Pineapple Coconut Pie

3 eggs
1 cup sugar
1/4 cup crushed pineapple, drained
1/2 cup white corn syrup
1/4 cup coconut
Juice from 1/2 lemon
1/4 cup melted butter

Beat eggs very lightly.

Add all other ingredients and blend together.

Fold into a 9 inch pie shell and bake in a slow oven, 300° for 45 to 60 minutes.

Pecan Cheese Pie

When we go out to eat it is rare that we ever order dessert. One day a new restaurant opened in town and after going there for dinner one of our girls ordered a piece of what was called Pecan Cheese Pie. Well everyone at the table was fighting for a bite. From then on we always got dessert when we ate there and it was always that pie. Well the restaurant was sold and the pie was no more, so I was on the search for a recipe to try and duplicate it. After a few, close, but not quite there tries, I finally came up with this. If you love pecan pie and you love cheesecake this is the pie for you.

1 deep dish pie shell

First Layer:
1 (8 oz.) package cream cheese
1/2 cup sugar
1 egg, beaten
1/2 teaspoon. salt
1 teaspoon vanilla

Second Layer:
1 1/4 cup pecans, chopped

Third Layer:
3 eggs
1/4 cup sugar
1 cup corn syrup
1 teaspoon. vanilla

Preheat oven to 375°.

Mix together the cream cheese, sugar, beaten egg, salt, and vanilla until smooth. Sprinkle all of the pecans evenly over cream cheese layer. Combine the 3 eggs, sugar, corn syrup and vanilla and beat until smooth. Pour over pecan layer. Bake 35 to 45 minutes.

Just Right Apple Pie

2 pie crusts

3/4 cup packed brown sugar
1/2 cup white sugar
3 Tablespoons of flour
2 teaspoons of apple pie spice
Pinch of salt
8 to 9 cups of sliced apples (I use a variety of different kind)
Juice from 1 lemon
1 teaspoon vanilla extract
2 tablespoons of butter

1 egg beaten
1 tablespoon of raw sugar (or white sugar)

Preheat oven to 375°.

Mix sugars with the flour, apple pie spice and salt.

Toss the apples with the lemon juice, sugar and vanilla.

Put the mixture in the pie crust and dot with butter.

Lay top pastry over the apples, crimp the edges and brush the top of the pastry very lightly with egg glaze.

Cut slits in the top and sprinkle with sugar.

Bake about 45 minutes or until crust is golden brown and apples are tender.

Amazing Strawberry Pie

We are also blessed with strawberries in our county. There are several farms where you can pick your own. This recipe is a great one to use when the strawberries are at their peak.

About 3 quarts fresh strawberries, divided
1 2/3 cups sugar
6 tablespoons cornstarch
2/3 cup water
1 deep-dish pie shell (baked)
1 cup whipping cream
1 1/2 tablespoons instant vanilla pudding mix

In a large bowl, mash enough berries to measure 3 cups.

In a saucepan, combine the sugar and cornstarch. Stir in the mashed berries and water; mix well. Bring to a boil over medium heat, stirring constantly. Cook and stir for 2 minutes. Remove from the heat.

Put in refrigerator for about 20 to 30 minutes stirring occasionally. When almost cool fold in the remaining berries and pour into pie shell.

Chill for 2-3 hours.

Whip cream until soft peaks form.

Add pudding mix and blend until stiff peaks.

Spread this mix on top of the pie.

Southern Pecan Pie

You really can't have a cookbook with southern recipes and not include a recipe for pecan pie. This is pretty much your basic pecan pie that has become a part of southern tradition. If you want to do something a little different try adding ½ cup of chocolate chips to the recipe.

1 pastry pie shell
3 eggs
1 cup sugar
2 tablespoons butter, melted
1/2 teaspoon salt
3/4 cup heavy cream
1/2 cup corn syrup
2 teaspoons vanilla
1 1/2 cups pecans

Preheat oven to 375°.

Mix the eggs, sugar, butter, corn syrup and salt together.

Whip the heavy cream for about 1 minutes and stir into the egg mixture.

Add the vanilla and the pecans.

Pour into the pie shell and bake for 40 to 50 minutes.

Moderation. Small helpings. Sample a little bit of everything. These are the secrets of happiness and good health.

—Julia Child

Million Dollar Pie

This is an old recipe that was a staple in the 60's at every homecoming and pot luck around. It's still easy and it's still good. Let's revive it!

1 pre-made graham cracker or cookie crust pie shell
1 can sweetened condensed milk
1/4 cup fresh squeezed lemon juice
1 large container whipped topping
1 can crushed pineapple (drained)
1 cup chopped pecans

Mix the condensed milk and the lemon juice until thick. Add to the remaining ingredients. Pour into crust. Chill. This will make 1 very large or 2 small pies.

Chocolate Mousse Pie

1 (9-inch) vanilla cookie crust
1 (14 oz.) can condensed milk
2/3 cup water
1 small package chocolate flavor pudding mix (not instant)
1 (1 oz.) square unsweetened chocolate
2 cups whipping cream, whipped

In a sauce pan, combine condensed milk, water and pudding mix; mix well. Add chocolate and cook over medium heat, stirring continuously until chocolate melts and mixture is thick. Remove from heat and beat until smooth.

Chill this mixture completely and fold in whipped cream.

Pour into cookie shell. Chill 4 hours or until set.

Grandma Lotha's Chocolate Pie

This is the perfect chocolate pie. Grandma Lotha made this pie for our family all of the time. I would never think of using another recipe for chocolate pie.

1 pre-baked pie shell
1 cup sugar
3 tablespoons cocoa
5 tablespoons flour
3 egg yolks
2 cups milk
1 teaspoon vanilla
1 tablespoon butter

Combine sugar, cocoa, and flour in a sauce pan

Add milk and stir over low heat until thickened.

Stir in the well beaten egg yolks. Add butter and vanilla.

Pour into pie shell.

Top with "Never Fail Meringue" and bake in 350° oven for 8 to 10 minutes.

Key Lime Pie

Lets not make things difficult if we don't have to. This pie is super simple, quick, and tastes fantastic. It's great after a big meal, especially seafood. Use key lime juice, not regular lime juice. It will make a big difference.

1 graham cracker pie crust
1 (14 ounce) can sweetened condensed milk
1/4 cup key lime juice
1 teaspoon grated lime zest
1 large carton frozen whipped topping, thawed

Combine the condensed milk, key lime juice, and lime zest. Fold in the whipped topping and mix thoroughly. Pour the mixture into graham cracker crust. Refrigerate at least 1 hour before serving.

Sweet Potato Pie

1 deep dish pie crust or 2 smaller pie crusts (do not pre-bake)
2 cups baked, mashed sweet potatoes
3 eggs
1 cup brown sugar
1 1/2 cups half and half
1 teaspoon cinnamon
1/4 teaspoon nutmeg
1/4 teaspoon salt
1 tablespoon molasses

* Note oven temperature changes.

Place the pastry in pie plate(s)

In a large mixing bowl, beat the eggs and the sugar until well mixed. Add sweet potatoes, salt, spices, half and half, and molasses. Blend thoroughly.

Pour this mixture into the pie shells.

*Heat oven to 450° and bake for 10 minutes. Reduce heat to 325° and bake it for 30 minutes or until the filling is set.

In a Pinch Fruit Dessert

On a Sunday night when you're just hanging out, relaxing, all of a sudden you really need something sweet and warm (and it's not your husband). Well I'll bet you have all of these ingredients on hand and this dessert is quick, simple and definitely a comfort food.

1 cup sugar
1 cup flour
1 cup milk
1 stick butter
1 large can of your favorite fruit in syrup or canned pie filling.

(Try peaches, blueberries, apples, etc.)

Preheat oven to 350°.

Melt the butter and pour into your baking dish.

Mix flour and sugar, add milk, blend well and pour over butter.

Pour fruit over the top.

Bake 30 to 45 minutes or until top crust is bubbly and brown.

Serve hot with vanilla ice cream.

Blueberry Delight

This is an old recipe that people have been making for years. It's easy and its good and it travels well. Plus it can be used as a side dish, salad, or a dessert!

2 sticks butter (room temperature)
2 cups plain flour
1 cup chopped pecans
3 cups powdered sugar
1 8 ounce package cream cheese
1 large container non-dairy whipped topping
1 can blueberry pie filling

Preheat oven to 350°.

Mix butter, flour and pecans. Press into bottom of a 9x13 inch pan.

Bake for 25 minutes. Cool crust.

Cream together sugar and cream cheese until smooth.

Fold in Non-dairy whipped topping and spread over cooled crust.

Pour pie filling over top. Chill before serving.

G'Ma Lotha's Whoopie Pies

If you were to have gone to my Grandma Lotha's when she was still with us and looked in her pantry, you would have seen several big jars of Marshmallow Fluff™. She always kept it on hand because everyone always begged her to make these cookies. I know several folks who requested that she make these for their birthdays, my Mama being one of them.

Cookies:
2 cups all-purpose flour
1/2 cup cocoa powder
1 1/4 teaspoons baking soda
1 teaspoon salt
1 stick butter
1 cup packed brown sugar
1 large egg
1 cup buttermilk
1 teaspoon vanilla

Filling:
1 stick butter, at room temperature
2 cups marshmallow cream
1 1/4 cups powdered sugar
1 teaspoon vanilla

Preheat oven to 350°.

Mix the dry ingredients in a bowl; flour, cocoa, baking soda, and salt in a bowl until combined.

In another bowl mix together the butter and brown sugar with an electric mixer until pale and fluffy, about 3 minutes. Add egg, beating until combined well.

Reduce speed to low and alternately mix in flour mixture and buttermilk mixed with the vanilla in batches, beginning and ending with flour, until smooth.

Put 3 tablespoons of batter per cookie, 2 inches apart onto two greased baking sheets. Bake until cakes spring back when touched, 10 to 12 minutes. Set aside on rack to cool.

Filling:
In a medium bowl mix together the butter, powdered sugar, marshmallow cream and vanilla with an electric mixer until smooth, about 3 to 4 minutes.

Spread a large dollop of the filling on the flat side of one cookie and top with another cookie.

Wrap individually with plastic wrap.

Mammy's Pecan Fingers

My Great Grandmother on my daddy's side, who we all called Mammy, always had these cookies around when I was little. They are definitely a southern classic and are still made regularly today for weddings and special occasions. Its Bobby's favorite cookie.

2 cups all purpose flour
1 1/2 sticks butter
4 tablespoons powdered sugar
1 teaspoon vanilla
1 cup chopped pecans
Powdered sugar for dusting

Preheat oven to 350°

Cream the butter with the sugar

Add the flour and the vanilla

Blend in the nuts and knead until able to form into 1 ½ inch to 2 inch fingers

Place on a baking sheet

Bake until brown, about 12 to 15 minutes

Cool slightly and roll in powdered sugar

Cookies are made of butter and love.

—Norwegian Proverb

Southern Pecan Cheese Bars

1 box Butter Recipe Cake Mix
3/4 cup butter
1 1/2 cups chopped pecans
1 cup brown sugar
2 8 ounce packages cream cheese

Preheat oven to 350°

Grease and flour a 9 x 13 baking pan

Mix the cake mix, butter and ¾ cup of the pecans together and press into the bottom of the baking pan

Mix the sugar together with the cream cheese until smooth.

Sprinkle with the remaining pecans

Bake for 25 to 30 minutes.

Granola Cookies

These are fantastic cookies! I started making them after my mother gave me the recipe when my girls were little. We either made these cookies or the chocolate chip cookies almost every week. I rarely bought packaged cookies and enjoyed being able to have the house filled with the aroma of baking cookies. It's just that little something special that you will enjoy making as much as everyone will enjoy eating. *P.S.* The 100% Quaker Cereal™ is sometimes hard to find but it's worth the hunt.

1 1/2 sticks butter
1 cup brown sugar (light or dark whichever you prefer)
1/2 cup sugar
1 egg
1 teaspoon vanilla extract
1 cup all purpose flour
1 teaspoon salt
1/2 teaspoon baking soda
2 cups of quick cooking oatmeal
1 cup Quaker 100% Natural Cereal™
1 cup raisins
1/4 cup water
1 teaspoon cloves
2 teaspoons cinnamon

Preheat oven to 350° degrees. Mix the butter, sugars, vanilla and egg. Add the flour salt and soda and mix well then add the cereal, oatmeal, water and raisins.

Drop by rounded spoonfuls on a greased cookie sheet. Bake 12 to 15 minutes.

Easy Pecan Praline Cookies

These cookies taste fantastic and are so quick and easy to make. If you need some cookies in a hurry for a bake sale or some unexpected company, this is your best bet. You just won't believe that something this easy to make can taste this good!

Graham crackers
1 cup packed brown sugar
1 cup butter
1/4 teaspoon cream of tartar
1 1/2 cups chopped pecans

Place the graham crackers in a single layer on large ungreased sheet pan,

Bring sugar, butter and cream of tartar to a boil.

Stir in the Pecans.

Pour mixture oven the top of the crackers.

Preheat oven to 325°

Bake for 10 minutes.

Cool and remove from pan while still warm.

Soft Chocolate Chip Cookies

1/2 cup Crisco™
6 tablespoons sugar
6 tablespoons brown sugar
1 teaspoon vanilla extract
1 teaspoon butter flavoring
1/4 cup milk
1 egg

1 1/2 cups plus 2 tablespoons of all purpose flour
1/2 teaspoon baking soda
Pinch of salt
1 cup of Ghirardelli™ Chocolate Chips

Preheat oven to 350°

Cream together with a mixer the Crisco, sugars, vanilla and butter flavorings, milk and egg. Blend this mixture until smooth.

Slowly blend in the dry ingredients.

Stir in the chocolate chips

Drop by tablespoonfuls on a cookie sheet

Bake for 8 to 10 minutes.

Peanut Butter Fudge

This is an easy fudge recipe that will work every time. No cooking until the soft ball stage and all of that stuff to worry about. You can use smooth or chunky peanut butter. We always have this at Christmas time at our house.

1   12 ounce bag milk chocolate chips
1   12 ounce jar smooth or crunch peanut butter
1   14 ounce can sweetened condensed milk

Melt the chocolate chips and the peanut butter over very low heat. When thoroughly melted remove from heat and stir in condensed milk. Pour the mixture into an 8 x 8 pan lined with wax paper

Put in the refrigerator and chill until firm.

Sauces, Dressings, Pickles, & Preserves,

*Those little "extras" that make things
just a little more special*

*"On a hot day in Virginia, I know nothing more comforting than a fine
spiced pickle, brought up trout-like from the sparkling depths of the aromatic
jar below the stairs of Aunt Sally's cellar."*

—Thomas Jefferson

The First Time I Made Grape Preserves

By Velma Harper Scott (Grandmama)
(Taken from her written story to me)

This happened soon after I was married in 1936. I had watched my mother make grape preserves so many times, and thought I remembered just how to do it. I picked the ripe grapes, washed them and mashed out the pulp, strained out the seeds and then added the rest of the hulls. I then went ahead and added the sugar (10 pounds to a peck of grapes!) and let them stand overnight.

The next morning I cooked them until they were preserved real pretty, and then I processed them in Mason jars.

At supper time, I proudly opened up a jar. Alton spread some on a nice hot biscuit with a little cow's cream and I did the same thing. Well, when we bit into it, those grapes were so tough you couldn't even chew them!

I learned later from my mother, that I should have cooked the hulls, juice and pulp with a little water until they were tender enough to cut with a fork and THEN add the sugar and preserve them.

I had to throw away my pretty jars of grape preserves and you can bet I really got laughed at, but I learned my lesson and never made that mistake again.

Mr. Larry's Crispy Sweet Pickles

(These Pickles take 8 days to make, so don't get in a hurry)

Cucumbers	Pickling Spice
Alum	Pickling Salt
Water	Sugar

Apple Cider Vinegar (Do not use white vinegar)

About 20 to 25 pounds of cucumbers will make 12 quarts of pickles. Use smaller, pickling cucumbers as they work better. If you only have large cucumbers, cut them in half and discard the seeds before slicing. Cut the cucumbers into ¾ inch chunks. (Try to stay consistent with your sizes.) These should not be sliced thinly they should be chunky.

1 st Day Put the cucumbers in a large heat proof glass or plastic container (Do Not use any kind of metal). Cover with boiling water.
2 nd Day Pour off the water and then cover with fresh boiling water. Add 1 ½ cups of pickling salt for each gallon of water used.
3 rd Day Pour off the water again. Then cover with boiling water mixed with 3 tablespoons of alum for each gallon of water used.
4 th Day Pour off the water. Boil enough apple cider vinegar and pickling spices to cover the cucumber slices. About 3 Tablespoons of pickling spices per gallon of vinegar.
5 th, 6 th & 7 th Day Rest. Don't touch them! Just forget about them for 3 days!
8 th Day Get another large pan and take all of the cucumbers out of the vinegar mixture. You can discard the vinegar. Completely cover the cucumbers with sugar. Let stand about thirty minutes. The sugar will start to dissolve and will make a syrup. Get your sterilized jars and lids ready. Pack cucumbers and syrup into the jars and seal. (You do not have to process these pickles)

The pickles will make their own syrup. Make sure the syrup covers the cucumbers in the jars. If you don't cover them they won't be crispy.

Note from Vicki

A wonderful family friend made these every year and gave us jars at Christmas. He is no longer with us, but we still talk about him and these wonderful pickles.

Grandmama Margie's Bread & Butter Pickles

This is a recipe from my great grandmother just as she had it written down. I remember these pickles well.

1 gallon cukes and 1 large onion cut up
1/2 cup salt
Use fresh cukes—wash and cut in thin slices
Do not peel
Cut onion in fine pieces and mix with cukes
Bury in water, salt and ice for 3 hours
Drain off water

Mix 5 cups sugar
5 cups vinegar
2 teaspoons turmeric
2 teaspoons mustard seed
1 teaspoon celery seed
1/2 teaspoon cloves, whole or ground

Pour mixture over cukes after draining off water
Place over low heat
Stir occasionally
Heat to boiling point
Do not boil
Seal while hot

Mama Tine's Sweet Pepper Relish

Bobby's mama, Mama Tine, always had this pepper relish on the table. We ate it as an accompaniment to just about everything.

12 large green bell peppers
12 large red bell peppers
12 large onions
4 cups sugar
1 quart vinegar
3 tablespoons course salt

Cut the peppers and onions up fine (or use a food processor) and pour boiling water over them.

Let stand for about 5 minutes and then drain.

Pour boiling water over again and let stand 15 minutes and then drain.

Have the vinegar, salt and sugar mixture boiling and pour over mixture.

Boil 30 minutes.

Ladle into sterilized jars and seal.

"The Canning Closet"

A closet in her bedroom, that had a sheet hung for a door, was the makeshift pantry for my Grandmama's canned goods. By no means am I talking about canned goods from the store. No, these were pint and quart mason jars full of the bounty from her summer garden.

When I was little that closet was one of my favorite places to play. At first, the lure that led me to the closet was a magnificent pair of red pumps. They were bright red, tiny and gorgeous and I loved them. I had never seen my Grandmother wear these shoes (and I never did). I think maybe she loved them too and couldn't bear to part with them, a memory from her younger days when she would dare to wear red pumps. Anyway, as I sat in the closet in my red pumps I became enthralled with the shelves at the other end of it. They were lined with beautiful colorful jars, full of all the vegetables she had grown in her garden.

Green string beans, yellow corn, the bright red tomatoes, shiny cucumber pickles and burgundy pickled beets. The colors were beautiful and the jars so clean and shiny. Sometimes I would carefully move them around and mix up the colors that she had so carefully separated. On the bottom shelf she kept her "sweet jars". Pears from a big old pear tree that she had been canning pears from since she had gotten married (the same tree that we still get pears from today). She made two kinds of pears, one in just a simple syrup, very light, and the other, her pear preserves, were a lovely dark amber and thick with bite size pieces of the chewy preserved pears. She made her fig preserves from the figs on the bush by the back porch that had big piles of oyster shells underneath it. She always had aluminum pie plates tied in that bush to scare away the birds. They loved the figs as much as we did. She also had a strawberry patch out by the road, so there was always luscious red jam, but my very favorite came from the huge scuppernong grape vine that was in the back yard. Those pint mason jars that glistened with almost black grape preserves, I thought they were just beautiful.

Grandmama would call me from the kitchen, "Bring me a pint of preserves to set on the table for dinner." She knew exactly what to expect. She smiled as I handed her a pint of grape preserves and sat down at the table dangling those red pumps from my little feet. We sat together, talking and waiting for Granddaddy to come home for our midday meal.

Fig Preserves

There was always a jar of these preserves in my Grandmama's pie safe. I can remember my daddy telling her all he wanted for Christmas was a couple of jars of her fig preserves. She had a big fig tree in her back yard so she was able to make a batch every year. Fig trees are pretty popular in this area and these preserves are common fare.

** If you have forgotten—A peck is equal to 8 quarts and 4 pecks equal a bushel.

About a peck of figs

Enough sugar to cover them (about 5 or 6 pounds)

Wash the figs and put into a large pot

Cover the figs with the sugar and bring to a boil. Cover the pot and set aside until the next day (Do not refrigerate)

The next day cook the figs on a low heat for about 2 hours

Seal in sterilized jars. Do not process.

Pear Preserves

There was (and still is I guess) a huge old pear tree in the back of one of my Granddaddy's fields. Every year we would go pick up the pears that had fallen and Grandmama would make pear preserves. The hardest part about this recipe is peeling the pears. The last time I did it I got a big blister on my hand from so much peeling!

Note from Vicki

You can also use this same recipe to make pears that will be soft and in a syrup, just don't cook them as long.

1 big 5 gallon bucket full of pears
Sugar to cover (5 to 8 pounds)

Peel, core and slice the pears into 1/2 to 3/4 inch pieces.

Put the pears in a large cooking pot.

Pour sugar over top and mix throughout the pears.

Cover and let this mixture stand overnight.

The next morning, bring the mixture to a boil, stirring carefully. You may need to add more sugar if the syrup is not covering the pears.

Turn down the heat and cook slowly, stirring often, until the pears turn a medium golden brown and the syrup thickens.

When the pears are preserved to your **desired doneness; put in sterilized jars and seal.

** The longer you cook the preserves the thicker they will get and take on an almost "candied" texture.

Scuppernong Grape Hull Preserves

My absolute favorite! Grandmama had a huge grapevine in her back yard and these preserves were a staple in our diet. You really don't see these preserves around anymore. I've never even seen them available in a grocery store or gourmet market. I have taken a little shortcut with the Sure-Jel™ and it does save a little time. Don't tell my Grandma.

About 4 pounds of scuppernong grapes
Sugar (see below)

Wash the grapes and squeeze the pulp out of the skins.

Set the skins aside.

Put the pulp in a large saucepot and bring to a boil. Cook at a simmer for about 10 minutes.

Remove from the heat and rub through a sieve to strain out all of the seeds then return the pulp to the pot.

Add the hulls to the pulp and bring to a boil. Simmer for 30 to 40 minutes or until hulls are nice and tender.

Add 1 cup of sugar for each cup of the cooked fruit mixture (one to one). Bring to a simmer and cook for 10 minutes. Add the Sure-Jel™ bring to a boil.

Boil hard for 2 minutes.

Remove from heat. Stir and skim any foam from top. Let set for about 5 minutes.

Pack into sterilized jars.

Apple Butter

Apple Butter was always something that we had a jar of in the refrigerator. If you have an abundance of apples it's really not that hard to make and well worth the little effort it takes.

About 6 pounds apples
2 quarts of water
1 1/2 quarts sweet apple cider
3 1/2 cups sugar
1 teaspoon ground cinnamon
1 teaspoon ground allspice
1 teaspoon ground cloves

Wash and core the apples and cut into small pieces (about 4 quarts)

Put the apples in a large cooking pot and cover with the water. Cook until the apples are very soft. Pour all into a large sieve to puree and remove skins and seeds.

Return the puréed mixture to the pot and add the cider and sugar. (You may add some of the apple pulp if you wish.)

Cook until thick.

Stir in spices and continue to cook until it is spreading consistency.

Pour into sterilized jars and seal

Note from Vicki

When cooking the apples put three marbles in the bottom of the pot and this will prevent popping.

Summer Strawberry Jam

This is so easy it's almost a sin not to make it when strawberries are in season.

5 cups finely chopped strawberries
7 cups sugar
1 box powdered Sure-Jel™

In a large saucepan mix the berries and the Sure-Jell.

Bring to a rolling boil. Add the sugar in quickly.

Keep stirring constantly and return to a boil for 1 minute. Remove from heat and skim foam off of top.

Ladle mix into sterilized jars and top with sterilized lids and tighten rings.

Super Simple Jam

And this is even easier but just as good.

About 6 cups of mashed fruit
2 cups sugar
1 large package of flavored Jell-O™

Mix the fruit with the sugar and bring to a boil. Boil for 3 minutes.

Add the Jell-O™ and boil for another 15 seconds. Stir well to make sure the Jell-O™ is dissolved.

Put in jars or glass container and keep in the refrigerator.

Dill Sauce

This is good to serve with grilled or fried fish.

1/2 cup mayonnaise
1/2 cup sour cream
2 teaspoons lemon juice
1 to 2 teaspoons sugar
1 tablespoon fresh dill

Mix all ingredients together and chill.

Red Seafood Sauce

You say cocktail sauce I say red sauce. Good with any type of seafood.

1 cup catsup	Juice from one lemon
2 teaspoons Worshtershire	2 teaspoons hot sauce
1 heaping tablespoon horseradish	

Mix all ingredients together and chill. (If this is too hot (or mild) for you, you can decrease or increase the horseradish and hot sauce.

White Champagne Sauce

This is out of this world on boiled shrimp. A great change from just having red sauce with them. I got this recipe from a friend of mine who attended culinary school. Just 2 ingredients!! (You can find champagne mustard at gourmet food stores).

1 cup mayonnaise
3 tablespoons of champagne mustard

Mix all ingredients together and chill.

V's Tartar Sauce

I have never purchased tartar sauce at the store. I always just throw this together.

1 cup mayonnaise
1/4 cup sweet or dill pickle cubes
1/2 teaspoon hot sauce
1 teaspoon fresh lemon juice
1 teaspoon chopped fresh dill

Mix all ingredients together and chill.

Homemade Vanilla Extract

As much as I bake I kept using up vanilla extract like it was going out of style. So I decided to make my own. Don't buy an expensive vodka for this, get the cheapest kind you can find.

1 fifth of vodka (use inexpensive)
3 whole vanilla beans split

Put the vanilla beans in the bottle with the vodka.

Close the bottle tightly and store in a cool, dark area for four to six weeks.

Remove the beans and discard. (or better yet put them in a container with some sugar and you will have vanilla sugar)

That's it. You now have a whole fifth of vanilla flavoring.

Blue Cheese Dressing

This is so much better than store bought dressing. It's easy to make, keeps well and is great not only served over a salad but along side chicken wings as well.

1 1/2 cups mayonnaise
1 cup sour cream
1 tablespoons lemon juice
2 teaspoons Worcestershire sauce
1 teaspoon hot sauce
1/2 teaspoon garlic powder
1/2 cup buttermilk (add more if you want a thinner dressing)
6 ounces blue cheese, crumbled

Mix all ingredients and keep in a jar in the refrigerator.

Will keep well for 4 weeks.

Easy Horseradish Sauce

This is really good served with cold roast beef.

1 cup sour cream
1/4 cup horseradish
1 tablespoon fresh lemon juice
1 tablespoon sugar
1 teaspoon fresh chopped dill
1 teaspoon fresh chopped parsley

Combine and chill several hours before serving

The Best Blender Hollandaise

1 stick melted butter
3 egg yolks, at room temperature
2 tablespoons freshly squeezed lemon juice
1/2 teaspoon salt

Put the egg yolks, lemon juice, and salt in a blender. Blend on low speed while slowly pouring in the butter. Serve immediately

Down East Sauce and Marinade

1 gallon vinegar
3/4 cup salt
1 tablespoons cayenne pepper
3 tablespoons dried red pepper flakes
1/2 cup hot sauce
1/2 cup brown sugar

Combine all ingredients. Use as a sauce for pork or chicken and also a marinade for pork, chicken and grilled vegetables.

Creamy Cheese Sauce

This sauce was the only way I could get my girls to eat broccoli when they were little. You can use whole milk in this recipe, but I find that using the evaporated milk gives you a creamier sauce.

1 tablespoon butter	1/2 teaspoon dry mustard
1 tablespoon flour	1 can evaporated milk
1/2 teaspoon salt	1 cup shredded cheddar cheese

In a medium saucepan melt the butter and stir in the flour. Cook over low heat for about 1 minute. Do not brown.

Whisk in milk, mustard and salt. Stir until smooth and slightly thickened. Stir in cheese and remove from heat.

Thanks for Sharing Sweet Tea with Me

I am blessed that my life has been so rich and fulfilling. I don't think I would be the same person had I been raised somewhere else. All of those life building lessons are learned when you are young. You learn to appreciate the things that are so very important. The things and the people that make you smile. The smells of the farmland and the river. The flavors of the food, the way it was grown and stored and prepared. Growing up saying yes ma'am and no sir and eating Sunday dinner at your Grandma's house. Those are the things that mold you and will stay with you forever. You will always appreciate them and yearn for them, even if you must, regretfully, leave our fair coast.

My love for cooking comes straight from that philosophy. Food is love in the south. Food revolves around everything we do. The recipes handed down from our grandmothers and great-grandmothers are sacred and we must not lose that connection with our past. I have shared some of those special recipes and remembrances of my southern roots with you in "Sweet Tea Please". So sit back, make a pitcher of sweet tea, and decide which one of these recipes you will try out tonight.

Best Wishes from the *Sweet Tea Girl*—

Vicki

Additional copies of this book may be ordered through booksellers or by contacting:

IUniverse
2054 Pine Lake Road, Suite 100
Lincoln, NE 68512
www.iuniverse.com
1-800-288-4677

or

Vicki Prescott
Sweet Tea Studio

www.sweet-tea-studio.com
252-249-0937

978-0-595-47299-4
0-595-47299-0